ENGLISH FREEMASONRY
AND THE FIRST WORLD WAR

ENGLISH FREEMASONRY
AND THE FIRST WORLD WAR

THE LIBRARY AND MUSEUM OF FREEMASONRY

First Published 2014

ISBN 978 0 85318 484 3

All rights reserved. No part of this book may be reproduced or transmitted in any form or by any means, electronic or mechanical, including photocopying, recording or by any information storage and retrieval system, without permission from the Publisher in writing.

© Library and Museum of Freemasonry 2014

Published by Lewis Masonic

an imprint of Ian Allan Publishing Ltd, Hersham, Surrey KT12 4RG.

Printed in England

Visit the Lewis Masonic website at *www.lewismasonic.co.uk*

Copyright
Illegal copying and selling of publications deprives authors, publishers and booksellers of income, without which there would be no investment in new publications. Unauthorised versions of publications are also likely to be inferior in quality and contain incorrect information. You can help by reporting copyright infringements and acts of piracy to the Publisher or the UK Copyright Service.

All images Copyright: The Library and Museum of Freemasonry, London

FRONT COVER First World War soldiers depicted on the doors of the Grand Temple at Freemasons' Hall, London.

BACK COVER Founder's jewel for Memory Lodge No. 4264.

PREVIOUS PAGE Sudan Chapter No. 2954 in 1910, with Kitchener in front row, centre.

CONTENTS

	Acknowledgements	*7*
1	The Masonic World in 1914	*8*
2	'Unprecedented Circumstances': The Impact of War	*16*
3	'A Permanent Memorial'	*34*
4	Prisoners of War	*46*
5	Aprons, Arms and Alms: Masonic Charity and the War	*60*
6	'The idea should be enough without trappings'	*78*
7	Post-War World	*84*
	Notes on Sources	*95*
	Bibliography	*96*

ACKNOWLEDGEMENTS

The Library and Museum of Freemasonry is located in Freemasons' Hall in Great Queen Street in London, a building dedicated to those Freemasons who died in the 1914-1918 war. In this book we have sought to describe events in English Freemasonry during that time. It is not intended to be a general history of the war but to tell the history of one institution and its members during that period.

The book has been written by staff at the Library and Museum of Freemasonry and draws on the extensive collections of objects, books, documents and images held there. Particular thanks are due to Martin Cherry, Mark Dennis and Susan Snell for their contributions. All the pictures in this book are copyright of the Library and Museum except the image of the ambulance financed by the Province of Cornwall on page 72 which is reproduced from *Thread of Gold: Celebrating the Unbroken History of 250 Years of Freemasonry in the Province of Cornwall* (2001) and is reproduced with the kind permission of that Province.

The Library and Museum would like to thank Dr Alan Borg and Dr James Daniel for their comments on parts of this book in draft form. Any errors are the responsibility of the Library and Museum.

Diane Clements
DIRECTOR
JANUARY 2014

THE MASONIC WORLD IN 1914

On the last day of January 1914, the District Grand Master of Madras, Sir Murray Hammick, a senior civil servant, travelled to Coimbatore in Tamil Nadu to consecrate the town's first Masonic lodge. Named in honour of the Pro Grand Master of the United Grand Lodge of England, who was also a former Governor General of Madras, Lodge Ampthill No. 3682 had to meet in the house of one of its members as there was no other suitable building. The founding Master was James Filson of the Indian Police but the lodge drew most of its members from the local Hindu and Parsee communities.

A week or so earlier and several thousand miles away, Major George Davie, the Provincial Grand Master for Devonshire, had consecrated his province's newest lodge at the Davie Hall in Plymouth. The members of the Sir John Hawkins Lodge No. 3704, named after the Elizabethan naval hero, then enjoyed a 12 course banquet at the Duke of Cornwall Hotel accompanied by a small orchestra playing light music.

At the beginning of January another lodge was consecrated in London, an addition to the 700 or so lodges already active there. Sir Edward Letchworth, the Grand Secretary, was accompanied by the Bishop of Barking as Chaplain at the consecration of Aetos Lodge No. 3702 in the Grecian Temple at the Great Eastern Hotel. They both received splendid jewels decorated with an eagle and a rising sun commemorating the lodge's name, the Greek word for 'eagle'.

The Masonic Year Book for 1914 'published under the authority of the United Grand Lodge of England' provided a snapshot of English Freemasonry. The United Grand Lodge had been formed in 1813, bringing together two English Grand Lodges both originally formed in the eighteenth century: the Atholl Grand Lodge, formed in 1751, and the original Grand Lodge whose formation in 1717 had marked the beginning of modern Freemasonry.

In 1914, the Grand Master was the Duke of Connaught and Strathearn, the third son of Queen Victoria. His involvement with Freemasonry continued a long association with the Royal family which had begun with the initiation of Frederick Lewis, Prince of Wales, in 1737. Connaught, an army officer, succeeded his brother Albert Edward as Grand Master when the latter had acceded to the throne as Edward VII in 1901.

ABOVE Portrait of Lord Ampthill, Pro Grand Master 1908-1935, by Sir Arthur Cope RA.

ABOVE LEFT Founder's jewel for Sir John Hawkins Lodge No. 3704, consecrated in 1914.

ABOVE RIGHT Founding Junior Warden's jewel, Aetos Lodge No. 3702, 1914.

Since 1911, Connaught had been Governor General of Canada and in his absence his Masonic duties were undertaken by Arthur, second Lord Ampthill, as Pro Grand Master and Sir Frederick Halsey as Deputy Grand Master. Amongst other senior office holders were Viscount Milner, a former governor of the Cape Colony, Michael Hicks Beach MP, a former Chancellor of the Exchequer and Henry Kemble Southwell, later Bishop of Lewes. Almost all of the 47 provincial rulers were peers of the realm including the Earl of Mount Edgcumbe who had been Provincial Grand Master of Cornwall since 1872, and the Earl of Derby, Provincial Grand Master of East Lancashire since 1899.

There were more than 1,700 lodges meeting across England and Wales. Their buildings were notable landmarks in many towns and cities. Local Freemasons were closely involved with their local communities fundraising for good causes such as hospitals, orphanages and church restoration. In April 1914 the Earl of Dartmouth, the Provincial Grand Master of Staffordshire, laid the foundation stone of St Mark's Church, Basford. The Bishop of Lichfield was present as well as 'a crowded audience', according to the report in *The Freemason*. Dartmouth remarked that it was the ninth such ceremony he had undertaken in 20 years. Amongst the numerous other public foundation stone-layings by Freemasons in the early twentieth century were the Gordon Home for Boys in Nottingham (1903), the Church of England Soldiers' Institute at Aldershot and the Commercial Travellers' School at Pinner (both 1904), the Nurses' Home at

West Bromwich (1905), the Chapter House of Liverpool Cathedral and Bury Grammar School (both 1906), the Royal Berkshire Hospital in Reading (1911) and St James' Church, Clacton (1912).

In the years before 1914, the English Grand Lodge was establishing about 70 new lodges each year. The jurisdiction of English Freemasonry extended not just over the 1,700 lodges throughout England and Wales but, as shown by the events in January 1914, also to a further 1,300 lodges located across the British Empire and its trading partners from Uruguay to Nova Scotia, throughout Africa from Egypt to the Cape, across the Indian subcontinent to China and south to New Zealand. There were 19 English lodges in Argentina and other lodges in Constantinople, Curaçao, Fiji and Zante.

As British colonies had become independent, they established their own Masonic jurisdiction or Grand Lodge. Informal links were established by the founding of 'imperial lodges'. Empire Lodge No. 2108, founded in London in 1885, was to strengthen 'the bonds that unite the Dominions with the Mother Country, by bringing the Brethren from Overseas into close relationship with Freemasons in the Metropolis of the Empire'. Within a year there were over 130 members representing 20 colonies and Canada. Its success encouraged the formation of Empress Lodge No. 2581 (1885), Anglo-Colonial Lodge No. 3175 in 1906 and the Royal Colonial Institute Lodge No. 3556 in 1912. Other lodges drew their membership from men connected with a particular country, dominion or colony. Canada Lodge No. 3527 was formed in London in 1911 as 'a bond of union between the Brethren of the Dominion and the Brethren of the United Kingdom'.

English Freemasonry was ubiquitous, respectable and, as with many other institutions at the time, facing the issue of women's rights. The English Grand Lodge had always restricted membership to men. From the late 1800s, the idea of extending the vote to women and ensuring more equal civic and legal rights had

ABOVE Portrait of HRH the Duke of Connaught, Grand Master 1901-1938, by Sir Arthur Cope RA.

been gaining ground across Europe. Political campaigning on this issue in Britain had become increasingly militant when, in June 1913, Emily Wilding Davison stepped out in front of the King's horse in the Epsom Derby and sustained injuries which led to her death. In 1882, Maria Deraismes was initiated as an equal member in an otherwise all-male French lodge near Paris. She established a new Grand Lodge which allowed both men and women to be members and which, in 1902, sanctioned the formation of a Grand Lodge for men and women in London. In

ABOVE Masonic parade at the foundation stone-laying of the Royal Berkshire Hospital in Reading, 1911.

1908, Dr William Cobb and others seceded from this to form the Honourable Fraternity of Antient Masonry (HFAM). Many of the men who joined Cobb's new organisation were members of English lodges, including the clergyman Frederick Gilby and Reginald Halsey, the son of the Deputy Grand Master, who was married to a prominent member of the HFAM, Marion Lindsay Halsey. In 1910, the English Grand Lodge issued a directive forbidding its members to join mixed lodges.

In the eighteenth century, Freemasonry had spread from Britain across Europe to France, the Netherlands, the German states and Scandinavia where self-governing Grand Lodges were established. The development of nation states and empires across the continent in the century after the fall of Napoleon in 1815, encouraged the consolidation of existing Grand Lodges and the formation of new ones in emerging states. In France and Italy, Freemasons often identified themselves with more progressive political causes and in both countries anticlericalism became a prominent feature of Freemasonry.

In 1877, the Grand Orient de France changed its constitutions so as to remove belief in a Supreme Being as a requisite for membership. This was unacceptable to the English Grand Lodge, which broke off Masonic communications with France. When several other Grand Lodges followed the decision of the French Grand Orient, European Freemasonry became divided between the English approach (also followed by Scotland

and Ireland and the American Grand Lodges) and what contemporaries called the 'Latin Masonry' of the Grand Orient. Representatives of Latin Masonry were also particular advocates of internationalism, beginning in 1889 when the Grand Orient de France convened the first of a series of international Masonic congresses. In 1902, the congress at Geneva established an International Bureau for Masonic Affairs based at the Swiss lodge, Alpina. The English Grand Lodge did not participate.

By the end of the first decade of the twentieth century, this period of splendid Masonic isolation was coming to a close. Although the Grand Lodge of England kept its distance from the various international initiatives promoted by the International Bureau of Masonic Affairs, it did permit an element of informal international fraternisation under the auspices of the Anglo-Foreign Lodges Association in London. Lodges established under the English Constitution included several which undertook their Masonic activities in languages other than English. The oldest of these lodges was Pilgrim Lodge No. 238, using German, which had been established in London in 1779. Lodge La France No. 2060 was formed in 1884, partly as a response to the breakdown in Masonic relations with the Grand Orient. Lodge Italia No. 2687 and Lodge L'Entente Cordiale No. 2796 were both formed in the 1890s. Deutschland Lodge No. 3315 was formed in 1908.

In 1904, Major John Woodall formed an International Masonic Club for the members of these lodges. The formation of America Lodge No. 3368 in 1909 prompted one of its founders, Frederick Conkling Van Duzer, to take this further and he proposed the formation of the Association. His vision for it included the promotion of 'the cause of Peace throughout the Earth'. The Association first met on 10 March 1910 and the meeting was attended by Ampthill, Halsey and fifty Grand Officers and Stewards. A five page report in *The Freemason* on 19 March included the headline 'Cosmopolitan Freemasonry'. The Association met annually until 1914.

Although the major German Grand Lodges had also withdrawn their recognition of the Grand Orient, relations between London and Berlin were not well developed. In May 1913, Ampthill, who was a fluent German speaker as the son of the first British Ambassador to the newly established German Empire, led a party of senior English Freemasons on an unprecedented week-long visit to Berlin at the invitation of the three Prussian lodges. The visit was widely reported in the Masonic press of the time and at the meeting of Grand Lodge in June 1913, which concluded that 'Masonic relations between England and Germany (have been put) on a new and firmer basis, from which incalculable mutual advantage may be derived'.

In December 1913 and after several years of discussion the English Grand Lodge recognised the newly formed *Grande Loge Nationale Indépendante et Regulière pour la France et les Colonies Françaises* in France.

International relations between Masonic bodies were formal. Grand Lodges 'recognised' each other

 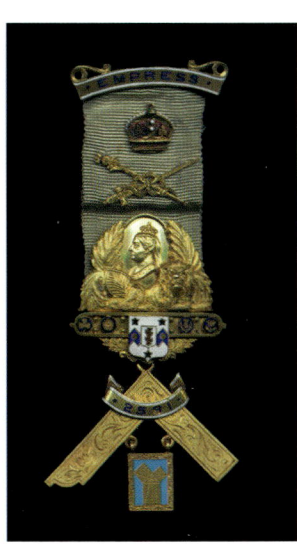

ABOVE LEFT Member's jewel, Santa Rosa Lodge No. 3579, established in 1912 in Buenos Aires, Aregentina.

ABOVE RIGHT Past Master's jewel for Empress Lodge No. 2581 showing Queen Victoria, a lion and palm leaves, with the shamrock, rose, thistle and daffodil representing the four countries of the United Kingdom.

and this created an official relationship which often led to an exchange of representatives. The United Grand Lodge had made provision for this as early as 1815 and by the 1880s the rule was established that:

> the Grand Master may…appoint any Brother to represent him in a sister Grand Lodge, and may constitute him and also any Brother, regularly deputed from a sister Grand Lodge, a member of the Grand Lodge of England, with such rank as the Grand Master may deem appropriate.

The names of these representatives were printed in the Masonic Year Book. The Masonic Year Book for 1914 listed all the overseas Grand Lodges which were recognised including (in the Eastern Hemisphere) those in Germany, France, Hungary, Italy, Denmark, Sweden and Greece; and, in the Western Hemisphere, Grand Lodges in the United States, Canada and throughout South America.

The war which began in the summer of 1914 was the first general European conflict since the fall of Napoleon in 1815. Its immediate cause was the assassination of Archduke Franz Ferdinand, heir to the Austro-Hungarian throne, in Sarajevo on 28 June 1914 by a member of a Serbian Nationalist secret society. This triggered a series of responses by European governments which had formed into two opposing alliances: Austria-Hungary and Germany

BELOW International Bureau for Masonic Affairs, advertised in *The Freemasons' Chronicle* in 1914.

ABOVE Medal marking the visit of Lord Ampthill to the Old Prussian Grand Lodges, 1913.

ABOVE Photograph of Sir Alfred Robbins, President of the Board of General Purposes, 1913-31.

on one side and the Triple Entente between Britain, France and Russia on the other. Austria-Hungary issued a lengthy list of demands to the Serbian government, subsequently declared Serbia's response to this ultimatum unsatisfactory and declared war on Serbia on 28 July 1914. Russia, bound by treaty to Serbia, announced mobilisation of its vast army and Germany, allied to Austria-Hungary by treaty, declared war on Russia on 1 August. France, bound by treaty to Russia, found itself at war against Germany and, by extension, Austria-Hungary following a German declaration on 3 August. Germany launched an invasion of Belgium in order to reach Paris by the shortest possible route. Britain allied to France, declared war against Germany on 4 August. Britain was also obligated to defend neutral Belgium by the terms of the Treaty of London (1839). Like France, Britain was by extension also at war with Austria-Hungary.

For Sir Alfred Robbins, 'the Prime Minister of Freemasonry' and the new President of the Board of General Purposes, the events of August 1914 'presented problems of unprecedented delicacy and difficulty to Freemasons' Hall – Britain's international allies were not Masonic allies'. It was just one of the ways in which 'the foundations of the earth were shaken' as English Freemasonry began to feel the impact of war.

'UNPRECEDENTED CIRCUMSTANCES': THE IMPACT OF WAR

The Supreme Grand Chapter of England, the governing body for the Royal Arch degree, met for one of its regular convocations at Freemasons' Hall in Great Queen Street, London, on 5 August 1914, the day after Britain declared war. Sir Frederick Halsey, as acting First Grand Principal, opened proceedings with reference to the 'unprecedented circumstances under which we meet today'.

By the time that the Grand Lodge itself met on 2 September 1914 with Halsey again presiding, the German army had already beaten Russian forces at the Battle of Tannenberg on the Eastern Front. Although the French and British armies had delayed the German advance in the south of Belgium, their success at the first Battle of the Marne was still not certain. Alfred Robbins, who was present at the meeting, later described the atmosphere: 'The hour was fraught with fate, not only for the British Empire and her Allies but for all that English Masons held dear… darkness was descending on many a soul.'

Calls for lodges to cease meeting were dismissed by Grand Lodge, but the two lodges with the closest German links, Pilgrim Lodge No. 238 and Deutschland Lodge No. 3315, did close. Members of both lodges had been faced with the provisions of the Alien Restrictions Act passed in August 1914, which had given all enemy aliens not of military age a matter of days to leave the country and forced all those remaining to register with the police. Several members of Pilgrim Lodge had left Britain by the end of 1914. As a consequence of the Act, over 10,000 civilians had been interned by the British government by the end of September.

In December 1914, the British government appointed a committee to investigate charges that German soldiers had committed widespread atrocities during their invasion of Belgium.

A general anti-German sentiment which prompted the formation of this committee was also growing within Freemasonry. Prince Frederick William Lodge No. 753 wrote to the Grand Secretary in January 1915, informing him that the lodge had voted to change its name to Ethical Lodge rather than be named after a German emperor. They replaced the imperial Prussian eagle on their Past Master's jewel with a female figure holding a banner representing

ABOVE Freemasons' Hall, London c. 1914.

'UNPRECEDENTED CIRCUMSTANCES': THE IMPACT OF WAR

ABOVE Recruitment advertisement in *The Freemason*, August 1914.

RIGHT Portrait of Sir Frederick Halsey, Deputy Grand Master, 1903-26.

knowledge with virtue. At a meeting of Royal Warrant Holder's Lodge No. 2789 that same month, members voted to 'exclude' (expel) Daniel Mayer, a leading theatrical impresario who had helped found the lodge and had been its first Master. Mayer was born in Germany in 1856 but had been resident in England since 1858 and was a naturalised British citizen. The Lodge Secretary, William Wise, explained that if he were to be reinstated a large proportion of the other members would resign. At the same time another member of the lodge, Ernest Callard, a company director and Past Master of Royal Naval Lodge No. 59, circulated a letter calling for all brethren of German nationality to be excluded from English lodges. One of his four sons, Malcolm Ernest Callard, had joined his father's lodge in 1908. After serving in the army in South Africa in the early 1900s, he spent five years in Malaysia as a planter and rejoined his regiment at the outbreak of war. He was sent to France as a machine-gun officer and was killed in January 1915. Another son, Stanley Edwyn Callard, died in France in April 1915.

ABOVE Past Master's jewel for Deutschland Lodge No. 3315, presented to Max Seiflow in 1910.

ABOVE Past Master's jewels for Ethical (Prince Frederick William) Lodge No. 753.

ABOVE Past Master's jewel for Royal Warrant Holder's Lodge No. 2789, belonging to William Wise.

As Robbins was later to write 'the higher authorities …had reason to believe that they could prevent Freemasonry becoming as a body directly entangled with the war', arguing that English Freemasonry did not involve itself with politics. But, following the sinking of the RMS *Lusitania* in May 1915, with the loss of over 1,000 civilian lives, and the publication of Lord Bryce's report five days later which concluded that the German armies had committed atrocities, anti-German feeling became 'overwhelming'. There were riots in London in mid-May. A week after the loss of the *Lusitania*, Robbins wrote to both Ampthill and Halsey:

> The uprising of public opinion on the aliens question this week, as evidenced not only in parliament but in every social circle… constrains me to the conclusion that the rulers of the Craft should make a definite pronouncement.
>
> We have striven at Freemasons' Hall for months, and, on the whole, with success, to prevent sporadic outbreaks on the matter, but it has now risen to danger point, and, unless the rulers of the Craft meet the situation frankly and at once, Grand Lodge may be swept off its feet in a paroxysm of passion, and much harm be done.

In June 1915 it was Robbins who proposed that 'all Brethren of German, Austrian, Hungarian or Turkish birth' should not attend lodge meetings 'in order to prevent the peace and harmony of the Craft being disturbed'. By June 1916 recognition had been withdrawn of all 'Grand Lodges in enemy countries'. The Grand Lodge was only one of many British institutions, including all the main London business and shipping exchanges, which effectively barred members of German descent.

Although the exclusion of enemy alien brethren was agreed, there were opposing views. The Rev. Canon Frederick John Foakes-Jackson, a Past Grand Chaplain, liberal church historian and Dean of Jesus College, Cambridge, was one of many who expressed

RIGHT Photograph by Carl Vandyke of Lieutenant General Sir Francis Lloyd.

concern that Robbins' proposal 'may be a departure from the fundamental principles of the Craft'.

A flurry of letters arrived at Freemasons' Hall from individual members who were affected by the decision. David Loebl, a member since the 1880s of the Lodge of Tranquillity No. 185 in London, whose son was serving in the armed forces, wrote that at his initiation, 'I was told that Masonry is universal and that there is no distinction between religion or nationality.'

Another long-standing member of the same lodge, Joseph Eisenmann – now known as Joseph Ellison – originally from Bavaria, resigned as the lodge's treasurer as 'a high ideal has become to me a severe delusion'. Khalil Jebara, a Syrian member of St George's Lodge No. 1170 in Manchester, stated that he had left Syria because of Turkish 'misrule'. His letter pointed out that the government had made a distinction in favour of naturalised subjects which the Grand Lodge resolution had not followed.

Germans formed one of the largest immigrant populations in Britain. The majority were in London but there were also German communities in northern cities. The textile industry of Bradford had attracted German immigration since the 1850s and, by 1914, a number of the lodges there had members whose surnames indicated German descent.

Several members of Pentalpha Lodge No. 974 were affected by Grand Lodge's resolution, including some acting officers. The lodge implemented it but sent a copy of its own resolution to each of the excluded members which stated 'this lodge regrets that it has the effect of excluding from Pentalpha Lodge certain members whose patriotism and Masonic worth are undoubted'. Two of the excluded members terminated their membership. Others anglicised their names and appear to have continued as active members of the lodge so that Edward Heilborn became Edward Hayburn and Arthur Sonnenthal became Arthur Wood.

The effect of exclusion was felt in English lodges across the world. Rising Sun Lodge No. 1022, the oldest lodge in Bloemfontein in the Orange Free State in South Africa, had 99 members in 1914. Four of these members were excluded including Ivan Haarburger, a local businessman who had been Mayor of the town in 1914. The lodge named after him in Trompsburg, about 70 miles from Bloemfontein, was renamed in 1916, taking the name of the town instead.

Oriental Lodge No. 687 had been established in Constantinople (now Istanbul) in 1856 and by 1914 was one of 23 lodges in Turkey established by foreign grand lodges. Its membership reflected the multicultural city where it was based with members of many different nationalities, including a small number of the local Turkish community. It met every month except during the summer period; its meeting on 2 October 1914 was attended by 15 members. The Ottoman Empire entered the war at the end of that month, on the side of Germany and Austria-Hungary, and the lodge ceased to meet, not reopening until October 1920.

In the years immediately prior to 1914, about 70 new lodges were being established each year, a reflection of increasing membership and the need to provide opportunities for advancement in lodge offices. Despite the dislocation caused by the war, between 20 and 30 new lodges were established each year between 1914 and 1917. Eighty five new lodges were established in 1918 rising to 129 in 1919.

The war effort itself provided opportunities to form new lodges. Two of the earliest wartime lodges were both in London: the City of London National Guard Lodge No. 3757, in 1915, and the City of London Red Cross Lodge No. 3781, in 1916. The support for the first of these was an expression of patriotic Freemasonry. The petition listed 283 founders and the consecration in November 1915 was attended by over 600, including the Lord Mayor of London. At the banquet following the installation of its second

RIGHT Circular about the founding of City of London National Guard Lodge No. 3757.

The City of London National Guard
VOLUNTEER CORPS.

74, Elfindale Road,

Herne Hill, S.E.,

1st July, 1915.

Re PROPOSED FREEMASONS' LODGE.
FORMATION COMMITTEE.

Col. G. T. B. COBBETT, *V.D.*, Regimental Commandant.

Sheriff H. C. DeLafontaine	Alderman C. A. Hanson
George Hughes	A. Burnett Brown
Oswald N. Bell	Major Louis A. Newton
Rev. Dr. H. G. Rosedale	R. S. Chandler
J. S. Granville Grenfell	W. O. Welsford
Dr. R. Poulter	R. J. Godson
Dr. W. Hammond	L. G. Cook
Dr. Felkin	C. Fastnedge
R. V. Vassar-Smith	W. Yeo

Dear Sir,

I am desired to inform you that it has been decided to form a Lodge of Freemasons in connection with the City of London National Guard. The object of the Lodge is to increase the *esprit de corps* already existing amongst the members, and it is therefore hoped that every Freemason in the Guard may find it convenient and agreeable to become a Founder of the proposed Lodge.

For the information of the members who are Freemasons I append the following particulars:—

1. The Lodge to be called "The City of London National Guard Lodge."
2. The Founder's Fee to be £2 2s. 0d., to include the cost of the Founder's Jewel.
3. The Annual Subscription to be £1 5s. 0d., to include the cost of the dinner (exclusive of wine) at each Meeting.
4. Membership to be restricted to members of the City of London National Guard.
5. The Lodge to meet at the Freemasons' Hall, Great Queen Street, W.C., on the last Thursday in November, February and May.
6. The first Officers to be Grand Officers, with the exception of the Senior Warden, which Office will be filled by the Reg. Commandant, Col. Cobbett, *V.D.*, but it is understood that the Officers will be entirely changed each year, except in any special case.
7. The first Master to be Sheriff H. C. de Lafontaine.
8. The Initiation Fee to be £10 10s. 0d., and the Joining Fee £2 2s. 0d.

Members of the City of London National Guard, being Freemasons already registered under the Grand Lodge of England, who wish to become Founders, should fill in the accompanying form and forward it, together with a remittance for £3 7s. 0d., to me, at the above address.

Members who are Freemasons not registered under the Grand Lodge of England can become Founders by first affiliating to an English Lodge.

The List of Founders will be finally closed on July 31st.

By order of the Formation Committee,

LEONARD G. COOK,

Acting Secretary.

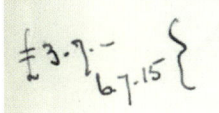

Master, Sir Francis Lloyd – who, as the General Officer commanding London District, was responsible for the defence of London – the large hall of the Connaught Rooms was filled to capacity. The first Master of the City of London Red Cross Lodge was Arthur Stanley MP, President of the British Red Cross Society. The founders were all attached to the ambulance column of the City of London Detachments of that society. During the banquet following the consecration there was a display of zeppelin 'relics'.

Many of the men who established Hendon Aero Lodge No. 3895, in 1918, worked in the aircraft industry in northwest London. Their working hours meant that they were often unable to attend their own lodges and the new lodge was established to meet in their free time on a Saturday afternoon. The lodge crest incorporated an aeroplane, a De Havilland 9.

In late 1917, over 80 men signed a petition seeking to form a Ministry of Munitions Lodge in London. The petitioners argued that men from across the country worked in the Ministry and many were, as a consequence, unable to attend meetings of their own lodges. The Ministry had been formed by Lloyd George in 1915 to improve the supply and quality of munitions. It had a staff of 12,000 officials.

Amongst the signatories were Winston Churchill, who had become Minister of Munitions in July 1917, another MP, Sir Laming Worthington-Evans, who was the Parliamentary Secretary at the Ministry, and Sir Leonard Llewellyn, the coal magnate. Although this specific petition was refused, many of the same men petitioned again a year later for a lodge to be called Armament Lodge. There were still links with the munitions ministry, but care was taken this time to make sure that the lodge was to be open to all. At its consecration in January 1919, the consecrating officers were presented with inscribed ashtrays made of silver which, together with that used to make the lodge collar jewels, was extracted from lead imported by the ministry for the manufacture of shrapnel.

The pressures of war meant that occasionally lodges were formed very quickly. Maguncor Lodge No. 3806 was consecrated within 15 days of its petition date in September 1917. It met at the Masonic Hall in Grantham, near the headquarters of the Machine Gun Corps, from which it drew its membership.

A small number of English-speaking lodges were founded in France between 1916 and 1918 and warranted by the *Grande Loge Nationale Indépendante et Régulière pour la France et les Colonies*. One of the most successful of these was the Jeanne D'Arc Lodge, formally established on 16 December 1916 in Rouen, a town with several permanent military establishments and one of the three main military hospitals. It met every week and on Sunday afternoons throughout the war, continuing to meet under the jurisdiction of the French Grand Lodge after the war when British members returned to London to found the Jeanne D'Arc Lodge No. 4168 in 1920. The ribbon colours of this lodge's early jewels were those of the French tricolour.

Several lodges with members on active service are known to have issued cards to their members which confirmed in four foreign languages, as well as English, that the holder was a 'worthy master Mason' and asked that any Mason who found him in distress or need provided him with 'brotherly care and lawful aid'.

The Masonic press reported occasionally on meetings held on the front line, but the surviving records seem to indicate that these meetings were essentially social events. At a dinner early in 1916, those attending from English, Irish and Scottish lodges had to finish their meal by candlelight due to the threat of a Zeppelin raid but nevertheless collected 14s 4d which was forwarded to the Grand Secretary. According to a report in *The Freemason*, in June 1916, a meeting of Masons representing more than 90 lodges serving with the New Zealand Expeditionary Force was held in France, 'within a short distance of the enemy lines and within range of his guns'. The opportunity was taken to mark Masonic occasions

'UNPRECEDENTED CIRCUMSTANCES': THE IMPACT OF WAR

ABOVE Founding Organist's jewel for Hendon Aero Lodge No. 3895.

BELOW Founding Deacon's jewel for Maguncor Lodge No. 3806.

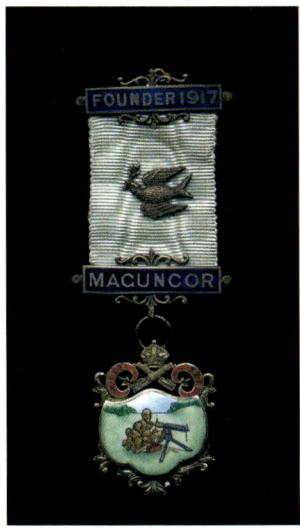

RIGHT Herbert Edgar Middleton, initiated in Maguncor Lodge No. 3806 in November 1917. After the war he moved to China, where he worked as an accountant.

such as St John's Night with a Masonic banquet held in Flanders in December 1916, involving men from Canada, England, Ireland, Scotland and South Africa.

In December 1914, Robbins reported to Grand Lodge that since September, 'the operations of the Craft have proceeded with vigour and success, though somewhat interrupted in the case of a number of Lodges by the absence of many of their members on active service and from other causes connected with the war'.

It was clear by now that the war was not going to be over by Christmas. One of the consequences of members' absence on war service was that they were often unable to pay their dues on time. This would usually mean being excluded from membership after a period, but Robbins announced a relaxation in this rule. The number of membership certificates issued to new members in 1914 (12,257) was only slightly lower than 1913, but by 1915 this figure had fallen to 10,133. This was the low point as the number of certificates then increased, reaching over 17,500 in 1918. The level of arrears and this (albeit temporary) fall in new members had financial consequences for Grand Lodge.

Grand Lodge's proportion of membership dues ('contributions from lodges') represented about 65 percent of its annual income and, in the years before 1914, total income (including investment income) comfortably exceeded expenditure and enabled the accumulation of surpluses.

Although contributions from lodges in 1914 remained at pre-war levels, Grand Lodge made several large donations totalling £4,000 to non-Masonic charities in the early weeks of the war and, as a consequence, its expenditure that year rose to £23,000 compared with the pre-war level of about £17,000 and, for the first time in many years, exceeded its income. In 1915, the situation was exacerbated by a 20 percent fall in lodge contributions. In June 1916, Robbins pointed out the effect that the war was having on 'central financial resources' which was 'necessitating the most careful watch upon expenditure in every

LEFT Founder's jewel for Jeanne D'Arc Lodge No. 4168, presented to Captain Creighton Nesbitt Jenkins.

RIGHT War Certificate and envelope issued to H.J. Wilkins by Aldershot Camp Lodge No. 1331.

direction' but the upward trend in memberships which began that year and was consolidated from 1917 meant that financial pressures eased.

In August 1914, the Defence of the Realm Act (DORA) gave the government emergency powers. It provided for censorship, imprisonment without trial and commandeering economic resources such as property for the war effort. By the early 1900s, many lodges had built or converted property for use as dedicated Masonic halls and several of these were now requisitioned for military use. Wivenhoe Masonic Hall in Essex, built in 1911, was requisitioned for an Army School of Instruction and subsequently for a 'Wet Canteen', a catering facility which served alcohol. The newly-built Masonic Hall at Frinton on Sea, a town where lodges only met in the summer as Frinton was a holiday destination, was requisitioned in 1914. It never returned to Masonic ownership as, after the war, it became Frinton Memorial Club, dedicated to returning ex-servicemen, and formed the town's war memorial.

On the outbreak of war, the Lodge of Faith and Unanimity No. 417 in Dorchester immediately gave its hall to the Dorset County Hospital for use by wounded soldiers and met elsewhere. In May 1915, the lodge protested at their premises being used for 'contagious and infectious diseases, or for enemy aliens' and held the hospital accountable for

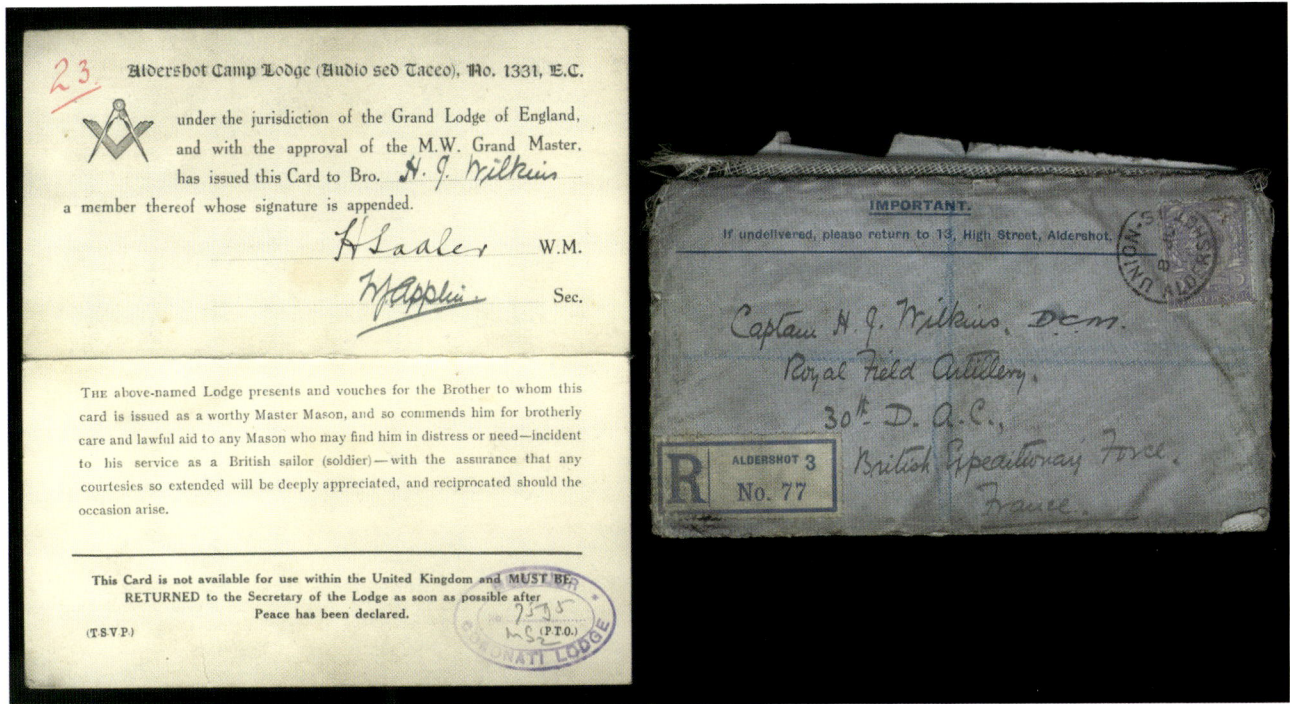

'disinfecting, re-decorating, and rendering the Lodge'. It was able to return to its hall in January 1918, having spent £100 on making it habitable.

Other lodges continued to meet in local public buildings or in hotels and inns. In Brighton, several lodges met at the Royal Pavilion. From late 1914, this was used as a military hospital for Indian soldiers and then, as the Pavilion General Hospital, for limbless men. The lodges had to find alternative meeting places. In Chelmsford, Springfield Lodge No. 3183 met in the church hall and, when this was requisitioned in 1917, had dispensation to meet in the local prison.

At the beginning of the war, three London lodges were meeting at the prestigious De Keyser's Royal Hotel on the Victoria Embankment near Blackfriars Bridge. In September 1915, the City Livery Lodge No. 3752 was consecrated and held its first few meetings there. The hotel had been established by Sir Polydore de Keyser, originally from Belgium but long established in London where he became Lord Mayor in 1887. As it was particularly popular with overseas businessmen, the war led to a collapse in the hotel's fortunes. In May 1916, it became one of many sites in London requisitioned for use by the War Office, in this case specifically by the Military Aeronautics Directorate.

The lodges all had to find alternative meeting places, with several of them using Freemasons' Hall in Great Queen Street at least for the remainder of the war. The dispute between the government and the hotel's owners about compensation later became a noted case in constitutional law.

On 16 December 1914 the German Navy attacked three seaside towns: Scarborough, Hartlepool and Whitby. The attack resulted in 137 fatalities and 592 casualties, many of whom were civilians. Old Globe Lodge No. 200 was meeting as usual that evening in Scarborough, but its minutes made no mention of it. The Masonic Hall in Hartlepool was slightly damaged during the raid but continued in use. Towns on the east coast continued to be subject to bombardment and, from 1915, attacks by rigid airships or Zeppelins. Springfield Lodge No. 3183 in Chelmsford took the precaution of paying three shillings to insure the lodge furniture against damage caused by hostile aircraft.

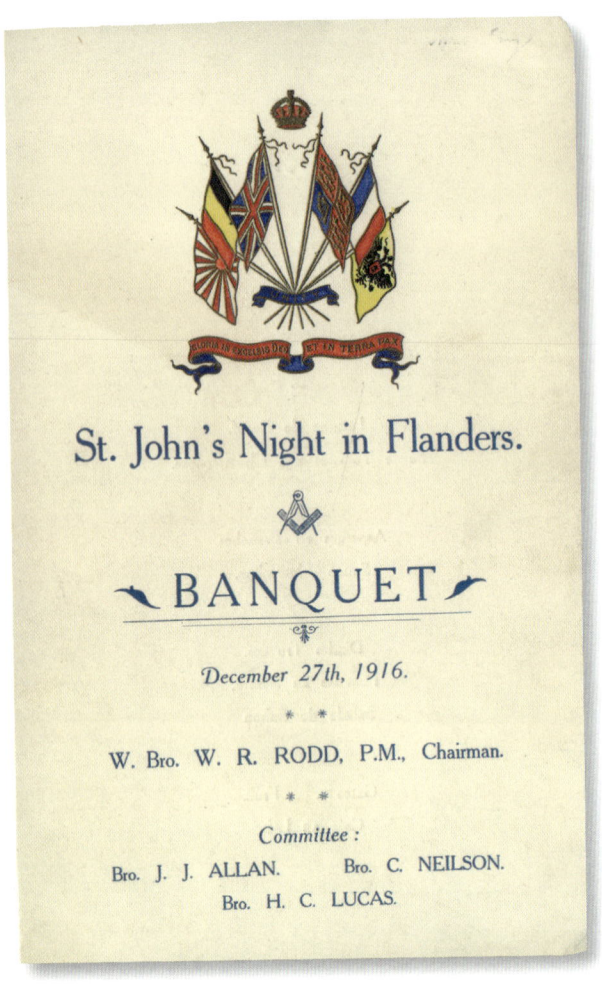

ABOVE St. John's Night in Flanders (27 December 1916) Programme.

By December 1916, Zeppelin raids had become part of life. The Girls' School at Clapham heard the heavy raids particularly in nearby Streatham and Bromley. During air raids, the girls were summoned by the fire bell to go with blankets and pillows down to the basement corridors. They particularly complained about Zeppelin raids on Sunday mornings; the raiders 'evidently know that on that day we have an extra half-hour in bed, and seem very anxious to deprive us of it'. The laundry windows had to be guarded with blinds to prevent glass damage but the school was hit by anti-aircraft fire in 1917, with a subsequent claim for damage costing £4 18s.

By 1918, almost one in four of the total male population or over five million men had joined the armed forces. The first lodges to be affected were those closely linked to men in the regular army or navy. By mid-September 1914, Lord Charles Beresford Lodge No. 2404, based in Chatham, Kent, had all its 250 members serving; another Chatham lodge, Per Mare Per Terram No. 3609, founded in 1911 for non-commissioned officers of the Royal Marines, had over 50 members on active service with only three remaining at home. Alma Lodge No. 3534 in Hounslow, whose members were drawn from the Royal Fusiliers, was also affected. Of its 45 members in 1914, 43 rejoined for war service; the lodge meeting scheduled for September 1914 did not take place and the lodge did not meet again until September 1918.

The Past Master's jewel for Aldershot Army and Navy Lodge No. 1971 shows an admiral in dark blue shaking hands with a general in a red uniform. The lodge was formed in 1882 for the 'convenience of the officers quartered in' Aldershot, Hampshire which by then was the 'Home of the British Army'. In 1914, there were about 150 members. All the principal officers of the lodge were sent overseas and only seven members and one visitor attended the meeting in October 1914. Although attendance dwindled to five or six at each meeting, two members, local clergyman Walter Williams and the Aldershot coroner, Sir William Foster, aged 70, kept the lodge active throughout the years of the war. The lodge also suffered nine casualties, including two honorary members, both Field Marshals: Lord Roberts who had died whilst visiting troops in late 1914 and Lord Kitchener who had drowned in 1916 when HMS *Hampshire* struck a mine. The annual subscription had always been kept low to encourage membership and was £2 in 1914. Arrears of subscriptions accumulated so that about £200 was outstanding at the end of the war; some of this had to be written off in the early 1920s.

Ionic Lodge No. 3210 in Bradford had about 65 members. Twelve of them saw active service including

RIGHT Past Master's jewel for Aldershot Army and Navy Lodge No. 1971, presented to Sir Francis Lloyd in 1906.

CENTRE Jewel for Arts Lodge No. 2751, with a sculpture in relief of George Blackall Simmonds.

FAR RIGHT Jewel of the New Zealand Masonic Association.

Harry Carter, silk manufacturer, in the Royal Flying Corps and Charles Blakey, bank manager, in the army. John Bland, a local wool merchant and a captain in the West Yorkshire Regiment, died on active service in January 1918, during his year of office as Mayor of Bradford.

The Masonian acted as a conduit for news between former pupils at the Masonic Boy's School and included reports of experiences on active service or as prisoners of war. Several old boys on leave visited the school and provided talks about their experiences, noting by November 1917 that 'familiarity with war has …bred contempt for its dangers'. One former pupil, L.B. Fox, a Corporal serving in 188 Company Royal Engineers, Gas Corps, in France, was involved in a gas attack on 25 September 1915. He reported, 'little did I think that my innocent experiments in the elements of chemistry at Bushey would ever lead me to make such revengeful uses of the gases of the 'fume chamber'.

The exploits of Captain and Flight Commander Percy Jack ('Pip') Clayson, who was awarded the Distinguished Flying Cross and Military Cross in July 1918 at the age of 22, also featured in the *The Masonian*. Flying in a single-seated Royal Aircraft Factory machine SE 5A, Clayson brought down 29 German planes and became the top-scoring air ace in No. 1 Squadron, based at Clairmarais, near St Omer, France. Others shared experiences of danger or being wounded on service worldwide. Sergeant C.G. Potter in the London Rifle Brigade, who was awarded the Military Medal in June 1917, was wounded in an attack on 20 September and was sent to a French hospital. While resting in a shell hole before dodging back to the allied lines, Potter thought the Germans had broken through and were attempting to defend themselves, but in fact they were surrendering and then helped to carry the wounded. He described his journey to the field ambulance, where he was given refreshments and inoculated against tetanus, before arriving at the casualty clearing station and travelling by train to hospital. He commented on the 'wonderful system for sorting out casualties, I eventually reached my Battalion Headquarters, and reported the situation, and was given a Scotch and soda (what bliss!) and cigarettes, and just before going to the Regimental aid post had a lovely cup of cocoa.'

F.C. Poulton, a Captain in the Army Ordnance Department, described repairing guns and the need to get close to batteries, his experiences of being shelled out three times and his travel arrangements by motor car and lorry. He described the long hours – 16 each day, seven days a week – and poor living conditions: 'when pitched, all tents now, as barns are nowhere to be got as we advance across the past 'no man's land,' noting that on occasion 'I have acted as doctor, adviser, and padre to my men'.

ABOVE Portrait of Sir Edward Letchworth, Grand Secretary 1892-1917 by John Dick Bowie.

The Military Service Act provided for exemption from military service in cases of ill health, serious economic hardship, essential civilian occupation and conscientious objection. This last exemption was invoked by about 16,500 men (0.3 percent of all men recruited or conscripted). Their cases were heard by tribunals which decided whether the objection was genuine and, if so, whether the exemption should be absolute, temporary or conditional upon some form of alternative service.

In March 1917, John Percy Cooke, a portrait painter and the secretary of Arts Lodge No. 2751, formed by members of the Art Workers Guild, wrote to the Grand Secretary about the lodge's decision to exclude one of their members, Arthur Glover. Glover, who was a sculptor aged 31, was a conscientious objector sentenced to six months imprisonment and then given civilian employment. He refused to resign from the lodge when requested, as he claimed that to do so would be to admit that he was wrong. Accordingly, two of the most senior members of the lodge, the sculptor George Blackall Simonds and the printmaker Sir Frank Short, resisting attempts by other lodge members to pursue a more conciliatory approach, insisted that Glover be permanently excluded from membership. Both men had lost their only sons during the course of the war.

Britain's declaration of war in August 1914 encompassed the British Empire, including Australia, Canada, India, New Zealand and South Africa. By early 1915, the District Grand Lodge in Madras was already commenting on the impact on local lodges with 'so many brethren having gone to the front'. One in ten of the population of New Zealand in 1914 – about one million – served overseas. Before the war, Canada had a small army of about 3,000 men, supplemented by about 75,000 part-time militia. By 1918, the country had over 600,000 men and women in uniform. The Canada Corps of 100,000 soldiers fought with distinction along the Western Front. In Canada, the Grand Lodges encouraged members to enlist in the Canadian Expeditionary Force, and to invest in war bonds to finance the war effort. The Grand Master of the Grand Lodge of Quebec declared in 1915:

> We are taking our part in the struggle as citizens of the Empire and as members of the loyal Fraternity which impresses on all its initiates the duty of never losing sight of the allegiance due to the sovereign of their native land, or of that in which they have made their home

In September 1915, in his speech at one of the last consecrations he performed, the elderly Grand Secretary,

Sir Edward Letchworth, noted that 'there never was a time in the history of Freemasonry more fitting than the present for strengthening the ties by which the Masons of the British Empire are bound together'.

Lodges across England entertained overseas troops and recruited them as members. In spring 1915, the Admiralty established a naval base at Poole and the local lodge, the Lodge of Amity No. 137 reported a record year for new members in 1915, with 11 initiates and seven joining members. The following year, the lodge resolved that all naval and military brethren in the borough of Poole be elected honorary members.

Those lodges established in London with imperial links were particularly active. In December 1914, Canada Lodge No. 3527 hosted a banquet for Canadian officers and, in October 1917, the installation of William Perkins Bull, the Canadian businessman and philanthropist, as Master of Elstree Lodge No. 3092, in Hertfordshire, was attended by a great gathering of Canadian officers in khaki.

At the outbreak of war, Grand Lodge had urged restraint in lodge meetings and in dining arrangements at festive boards after lodge meetings. The Grand Master set an example by not wearing evening dress at Masonic functions and many lodges began to dine much more simply.

In January 1917, the German government announced its intention to use unrestricted submarine warfare. Britain began to face problems of food supply and Viscount Rhondda, an industrialist and Freemason in South Wales, became Minister of Food Control in June 1917. Food rationing was introduced in January 1918 beginning with sugar and then meat. This prompted a Grand Lodge circular to all lodges, urging strict economy in the consumption of food.

The merchant service providing commercial shipping was particularly vulnerable to attacks by German submarines, and there were casualties amongst the members of many lodges based in ports. Losses in

ABOVE David Alfred Thomas, 1st Viscount Rhonnda, Minister of Food Control.

St George's Lodge No. 431, based in North Shields, included John Perry, aged 20, a mess room steward on the SS *Maindy Bridge*, sunk by a submarine off the coast of Sunderland on a voyage from Middlesbrough to the Tyne in December 1917, and William Carmichael, aged 60, who died the following month on the collier SS *Birtley* returning from Dunkirk.

In early 1917, submarine warfare and the sinking of American shipping in the North Atlantic together with the news of Germany's offer of a military alliance with Mexico, revealed in the decoded Zimmerman telegram, finally persuaded President Woodrow Wilson to end American neutrality. Congress voted to declare war on 6 April 1917. The first troops of the American Expeditionary Force arrived within a few months.

United Grand Lodge of England.

Freemasons' Hall,

Great Queen Street, W.C. 2

7th January, 1918.

Dear Sir and Brother,

At the Quarterly Communication of Grand Lodge, held on the 5th ult., there was adopted a report of the Board of General Purposes, two paragraphs in particular of which are desired to be brought to the especial knowledge of the Brethren throughout the Craft.

FOOD ECONOMY.

The first of these paragraphs was in the following terms :—

"Once more, and with even greater earnestness, because of the steadily increasing national necessity for the observance of strict economy in the consumption of food, the Board appeals to the Lodges in general and every Mason in particular to observe the utmost practicable abstinence in this regard. The M.W. Grand Master has expressed the earnest hope that the Craft in an especial degree will respond to His Majesty the King's appeal for economy and frugality, thus realizing His Royal Highness' sanguine hope that the Craft will set a good example to the Nation in this hour of her need. The Board fully recognizes and appreciates the efforts already made by the Lodges to carry out the Royal wish; and it trusts with confidence to the loyalty of the Brethren to both the Country and the Craft to redouble those efforts with considerable effect."

In supporting the motion for the adoption of the report, R.W. Bro. the Right Hon. Lord Rhondda, S.G.W., Minister of Food, said :—

"R.W. Deputy Grand Master and Brethren, the paragraph in the Report to which the President of the Board of General Purposes has just called attention, naturally interests me in a very special degree, holding the position I do to-day of Food Controller. It is quite unnecessary for me to make any appeal to Freemasons more than is made in this paragraph, urging them to observe economy in the matter of food consumption. It is a matter of particular gratification to me—of profound gratification, indeed—that this paragraph appears in the Report of the Board. I know it is unnecessary to urge Freemasons to set an example ; but I would urgently appeal to them to use their enormous influence throughout the country at the present time in the direction of food economy. I am only expressing my individual opinion, and not committing my colleagues in the Government, when I say that it is borne in upon me more and more that this war is going to be won by the self-sacrifice—even by the privations—of our people at home quite as much as by the great

ABOVE Grand Lodge circular on food control, January 1918.

'UNPRECEDENTED CIRCUMSTANCES': THE IMPACT OF WAR

LEFT Medal struck for American soldiers of the Overseas Masonic Club of Paris, 1918-19.

On 21 May 1917, British Lodge No. 8 held a joint meeting with the members of America Lodge No. 3368. The invitation card was headed: 'To commemorate the entrance of the United States of America into the War of Freedom.' Amongst those attending was the Reverend Dr Joseph Fort Newton, a Texan Baptist minister then based at the City Temple in London.

On Saturday 23 June 1917, 8,000 Freemasons assembled at the Royal Albert Hall to mark the bicentenary of the formation of the first Grand Lodge in 1717. The loyal address to the King, in the form of a telegram, included reference to the war in hoping that 'victory may crown your arms, and that a just and lasting peace may be the result'.

Amongst the many congratulatory telegrams and letters received from Grand Lodges and individual lodges were those from Freemasons in Palestine, from a Chinese Labour Camp near Folkestone in the name of Doric Lodge No. 1433 from Chinkiang and from the Freemasons interned at Ruhleben. The next day a Masonic service was held at the Royal Albert Hall, where the address was delivered by Henry Wakefield, the Bishop of Birmingham, as Grand Chaplain. Wakefield's address reflected his interest in social reform, calling for 'the England of to-morrow' as 'the home of fullest freedom' to reflect the influence of women and with an education system of the highest quality. He called upon members to 'apply the Craft to public life'.

By early 1918, the British government's gradual extension of eligibility for military service was causing problems for Grand Lodge at its headquarters in Great Queen Street. A relaxation in the minimum

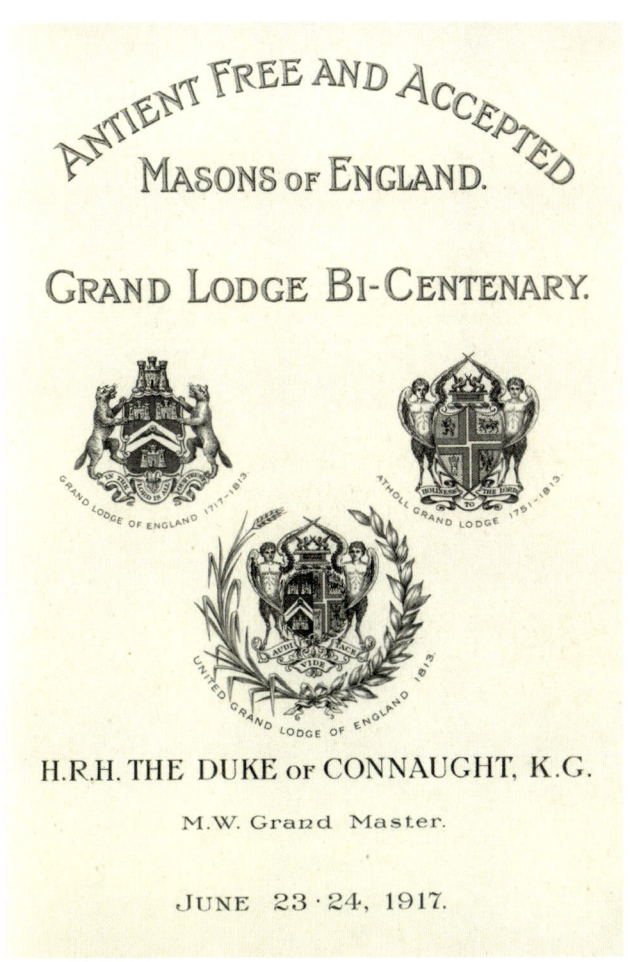

ABOVE Frontispiece of the programme for the 1917 events marking the bi-centenary.

qualification for employment in the Grand Secretary's office was agreed, permitting the employment of non-Masons and even women, a decision already taken by the Masonic charities. Philip Colville Smith, the new Grand Secretary, was able to employ Miss Gertie Haigh as 'personal typewriter', a role she had held in his previous employment as Secretary to the RMBI. By November 1920, the staff included six ladies.

The armistice came into effect at 11am on 11 November 1918. The first post-war meeting of Grand Lodge was on 4 December and Robbins took the opportunity to place on record its gratitude 'for the way in which Freemasonry has stood the strain of over four years war.'

'A PERMANENT MEMORIAL'

The idea of a Masonic Roll of Honour was first considered by Grand Lodge at its meeting on 2 December 1914, its second after the outbreak of war.

By this time, the first battles at the Marne and Ypres had resulted in the establishment of trenches along the Western Front while the latter battle saw total casualties of more than 250,000 men, including nearly half of the British Regular Army.

Two early casualties were mentioned at the December meeting: Field Marshal Lord Roberts, a Past Senior Grand Warden, and Prince Maurice of Battenburg, of Old Wellingtonian Lodge No. 3404 and Twelve Brothers Lodge No. 785, a lieutenant in the King's Royal Rifle Corps, who died in late October from wounds received in action at Ypres.

It was proposed that the roll should give the names of those brethren of all ranks who had laid down their lives in the service of their country, to be compiled on the basis of returns made by lodge secretaries. During the following year, the idea was further refined by the suggestion that it should 'form a permanent memorial of active patriotism displayed by Freemasonry in the momentous struggle still proceeding' in the words of Alfred Robbins.

A circular letter and a form sent by Grand Lodge to individual secretaries asked for name, military rank and Masonic rank. Secretaries were asked to record names of brethren known to have died or whose deaths, having previously occurred, had subsequently become known. The first deadline was 11 November 1915, a day and month which were to become highly significant at the end of the war but which were determined on this occasion by the requirements of printing the Masonic Year Book.

The first list appeared in the Masonic Year Book for 1916. It ran for 30 pages and included over 500 names, with each listed under his lodge. At first the annual lists were cumulative, until the 1918 Year Book which listed all casualties before November 1917. By this stage, the list of names ran to 105 pages representing over 15 percent of the book. For the next two years, only casualties notified in that year were listed.

The Roll of Honour continued to appear in each year book until 1920, when the final list covered the period from November 1918 until November 1919. Over 2,500 names had been recorded in the year books over the course of the war. By June 1921, the roll was declared complete, listing 3,078 names, and was printed in book form. Copies were also available for purchase.

One of the two weekly Masonic newspapers at the time, the *Freemasons' Chronicle*, had begun to print a list of casualties in December 1914. In addition to name, its list gave service rank, lodge name and number and details of the death. It also included names of casualties from Scottish and Irish lodges. By the second anniversary of the war in August 1916, its cumulative list of names ran to two of its total of 12 pages. With newsprint restricted, after this date only newly advised casualties were listed.

British casualties in the first three months of the war totalled almost 90,000 men. In August 1914, the government issued a call for 100,000 soldiers. By the end of September, over 750,000 men had enlisted voluntarily and this continued until, by September 1915, there were over two million enlisted men. The casualties recorded in the year books reflected this pattern of recruitment. The largest numbers of casualties recorded in the early lists were from those lodges associated with the regular army, the navy and the merchant marines. Lord Charles Beresford Lodge No. 2404, based in Chatham, Kent, reported 19 casualties by November 1915 and total casualties of 29. Two other service lodges – United Service Lodge No. 1428 in Portsmouth and United Service Lodge No. 3124 in Sheerness – each lost 18 members in the first year.

Apollo University Lodge No. 357, associated with Oxford University, regularly initiated new members under the age of 21 years, usually the lowest age for Masonic membership. Many of its members were early volunteers and over 50 names from that lodge were recorded on the Roll of Honour. Amongst them was John Norwood, who had been awarded the Victoria Cross for his actions in the South African War and died at the Battle of the Marne in September 1914. The other university lodge, Isaac Newton University Lodge No. 859 at Cambridge, recorded 16 casualties.

The two earliest casualties both died on 6 August, two days after war was declared. Both were from Plymouth. Joseph Gedge was a Paymaster in the Royal Navy and a member of Sir Francis Drake Lodge No. 2649; James Deacon was a petty officer blacksmith and a member of Queen Victoria Lodge No. 2655. Both were crew members of HMS *Amphion* which was sunk by a German mine in the English Channel.

Amongst other early casualties was Jonathan Knowles, a member of Pentalpha Lodge No. 974 in Bradford. A career army officer who had served in the South African War and in India and Burma, Captain Knowles went to France with the British Expeditionary Force and was killed at the Battle of Mons in August 1914.

John Sydney Paulson was initiated in the Lodge of Harmony No. 272, Boston, Lincolnshire, where his father was also a member, in April 1914. At the time he was an assistant master at Orme Boys School in Newcastle under Lyne, having graduated with a chemistry degree from the University of London. He had served in the London University Officers Training Corps and volunteered at the outbreak of war. Paulson left for France on 22 August 1914. He died during the Battle of the Aisne on 13 September 1914. Amongst the casualties lost when the RMS *Lusitania* was torpedoed on 7 May 1915 were at least seven crew members who belonged to Liverpool lodges including William Ruffels of Toxteth Lodge No. 1356.

Troops from India were moved to the Western Front and also served in the Middle East. Lebong Lodge No. 3321 had been established in 1906 at Lebong, near Darjeeling in West Bengal, one of the highest towns in India and the location for an army barracks which provided the membership of the lodge. Amongst its casualties were Lieutenant Colonel Aylmer Martin and Colour Sergeants George Muchall

ABOVE LEFT Founder's jewel of Lord Charles Beresford Lodge No. 2402.

ABOVE RIGHT Founder's jewel of United Service Lodge No. 3124.

RIGHT Title page of the Roll of Honour book.

MASONIC ROLL OF HONOUR

NAMES OF BRETHREN
who fell in the service of their
King & Country during
the Great War
1914–1918

FREEMASONS' HALL, LONDON, W.C. 2
1921

and Walter Black, who all died on the Western Front in 1915. Another member of the lodge, Joseph Slaymaker, died in Bulgaria in November 1918.

Over 540 names were added to the Roll of Honour between November 1915 and November 1916, a period which included the immense losses incurred at the Battle of the Somme in July 1916, amongst them, Harold Leslie Rayner of Apollo University Lodge No. 357.

The losses recorded from 1916 to 1917 totalled 467, including casualties from the Battle of Passchendaele on the Western Front (June – November 1917) and the period of unrestricted submarine warfare by Germany from February 1917, declaring a war zone around the British Isles which led to substantial shipping losses. William Havelock Jenkins, a member of Bute Lodge No. 960 in Cardiff, was a casualty when the coal steamer SS *Lydie* was torpedoed on her journey from Cardiff to Brest in February 1918.

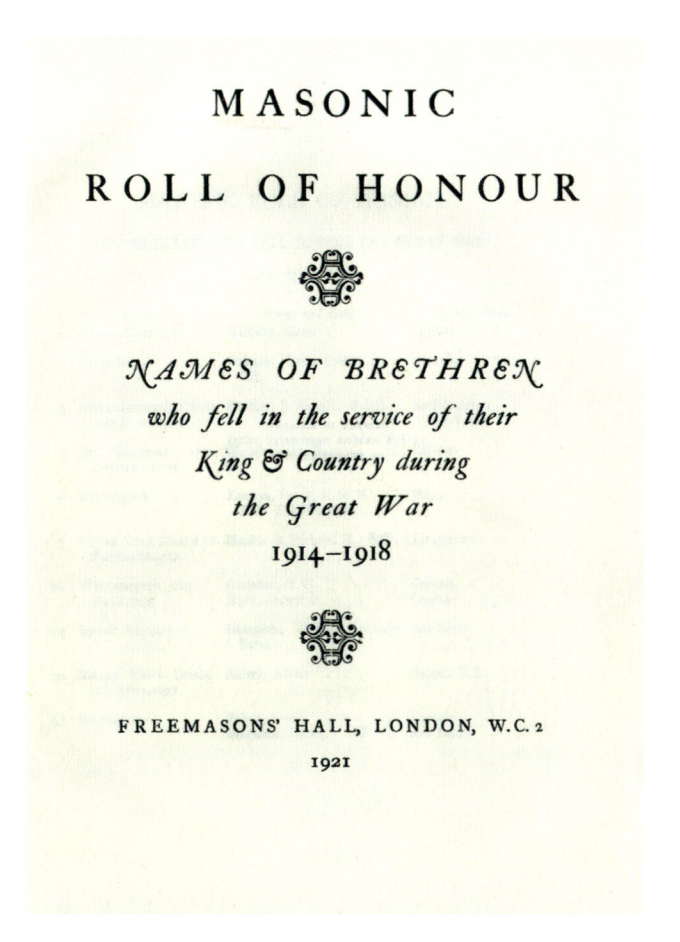

The largest number of names – 677 – was recorded for the period covering the last year of the war on the Western Front to November 1918. There were several instances of lodges recording the deaths of members of the same family. Ellesmere Lodge No. 730 in Chorley suffered the loss of Charles Critchley, a former bank clerk, who died at Gallipoli in June 1915 and his younger brother, Roland, a dentist who joined the Royal Air Force and died in April 1918.

In some places, fighting continued after November 1918 and demobilisation took some time, so casualties continued to be recorded – 380 between November 1918 and November 1919. A number of British troops were sent to Russia to support the White Russian forces against the Bolsheviks. Tristram Pine-Coffin, a member of Sir John Hawkins Lodge No. 3704, founded in Plymouth in January 1914, was listed as being in

RIGHT Title page of *Memorials of Masonians Who Fell in the Great War*.

FACING PAGE The entry for John Sidney Roberts in *Memorials of Masonians Who Fell in the Great War*.

the Intelligence Corps on the Roll of Honour; he was killed in action at Murmansk in September 1919. John Sidney Roberts, a despatch rider to Sir Douglas Haig, the Commander-in-Chief, went on leave to Paris late in 1918 where he contracted influenza and died in January 1919. Roberts had been educated at the Royal Masonic Institution for Boys and joined the Old Masonians Lodge No. 2700 in April 1914.

A former headmaster at the Masonic Boys School, Lieutenant Robert Stanley Chandler, who had encouraged many pupils to serve with the London Rifle Brigade, compiled statistics about former boys serving in the armed forces, recording details for about 750 Old Masonians. Of these 106 were killed, together with two house masters and four assistant house masters. In 1922 a book was published, *Memorials of Masonians Who Fell in the Great War* which gave biographical details of each casualty with a photograph.

The Boys School unveiled a war memorial to the fallen in November 1920, comprising an Ionic cross made of Aberdeen red granite on a circular seat of Portland Stone, situated opposite the clock tower of the school. It recognised that:

> The dead are but the chosen representatives of all our Old Boys who faced the sweat and blood and tragedy of the war… They have taught us that every boy in our school is a possible hero and have given us a new faith in our fellows.

The Imperial War Graves Commission was established in 1917, to undertake the reburial of the fallen soldiers of Britain and her empire in permanent cemeteries. Its work developed from the activities of Sir Fabian Ware with the Red Cross, marking graves which might otherwise be unrecorded. By 1918, over 500,000 graves had been identified, with an equal number of casualties registered as having no known resting place. The work of the Commission was based on two early decisions: that bodies should not be repatriated and that memorials should be uniform in their style. In the years after the war, the Commission worked to establish places of commemoration and mark, record and maintain the graves. Over 500 cemeteries were built in the 10 years after the end of the war, together with a series of memorials designed by some of the leading architects of the day. Rudyard Kipling joined the Commission as literary adviser; he chose the biblical phrase 'Their Name Liveth For Evermore' for the stones of remembrance on larger war graves

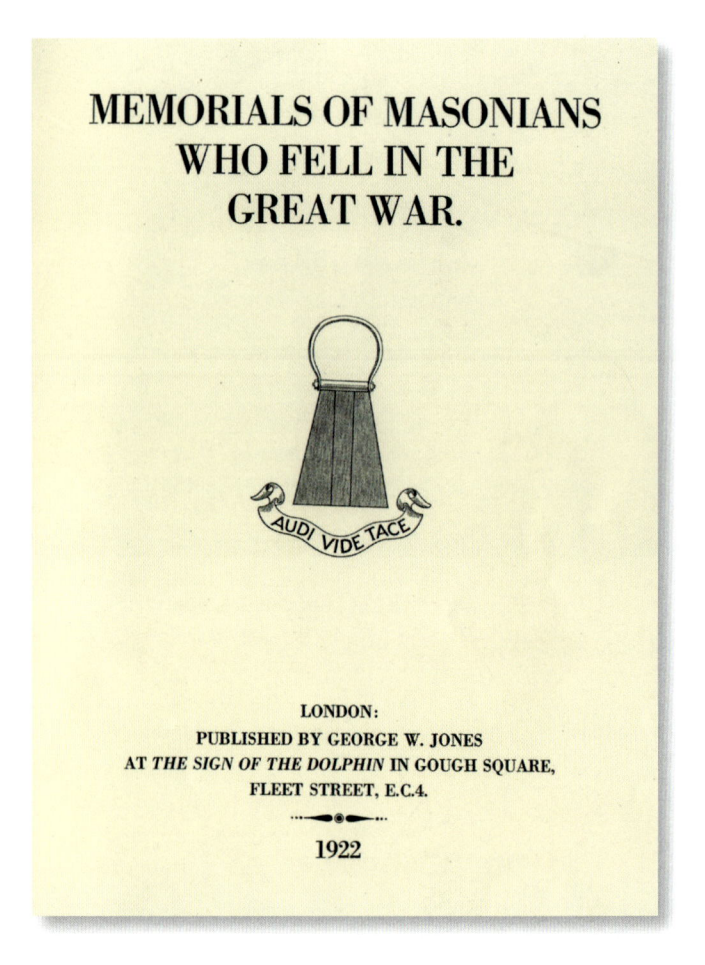

> **John Sidney Roberts.**
> Corporal, Motor-Cycle Section, Royal Engineers.
>
> Born 12 October, 1892.   *Burwood*, 1903-1908.
>
> JOHN SIDNEY ROBERTS, younger brother of the foregoing, joined the Army in August, 1914. He was attached to the Motor-Cycle Section, Royal Engineers, and his war service and experiences cannot better be described than in the words of Sergeant R. W. Gore, late R.E., who was in charge of G.H.Q. Despatch Riders from 1914 to 1919.
>
> He says: "Corporal J. S. Roberts joined the G.H.Q. Despatch Riders with the first batch of reinforcements after the first day of the Retreat from Mons. . . . He arrived one mile south of Landrecies the night after the 1st Corps' battle there, with a message for 1st Corps H.Q. He volunteered to keep guard that night, as he had had rest the night before, and most of the others had had none for two nights. He then joined in the general retreat to the south. He was soon a general favourite, his cheerful confidence and (alleged) knowledge of French assisting all of us to find our way. His enquiries usually began (and ended) thus: 'Dites donc, mon vieux, n'est-ce pas?'"
>
> Roberts had the reputation of always getting his despatch delivered and getting back with the reply. Occasionally the machine would break down, when he would hire or borrow a horse and get to his destination, after which he would return in triumph with his machine in a cart. What he lacked at first in knowledge of motor-cycle vagaries he made up in keenness and a solid sense of duty.
>
> After the victory of the Marne and the crossing of the Aisne, trench warfare began and the duties of despatch riders became more regular, and Roberts was stationed at St. Omer till 1916. For some time it was his particular duty to keep in touch with the Belgian H.Q. at La Panne, and for this purpose he was temporarily stationed at Bergues, by the inhabitants of which he became very well known and esteemed.

JOHN SIDNEY ROBERTS.

and the phrase 'Known unto God' for the gravestones of unidentified servicemen. He also suggested the inscription 'The Glorious Dead' on the Cenotaph in Whitehall, London.

In 1922, Kipling helped to found and name Builders of the Silent Cities Lodge No. 12 meeting at St Omer under the jurisdiction of the *Grande Loge Nationale Indépendante et Régulière pour la France et les Colonies* whose membership was drawn from the Commission. When the headquarters of the Commission moved to London in 1925, an English lodge of the same name, numbered 4948, was established there. Its first Master was Sir Herbert Ellissen, the controller of the Commission. Other early members included the architect Henry Cart de Lafontaine, who had been Chief Inspector of Works in the early years of the Commission, the lawyer Sir Henry Maddocks and the Canadian Colonel Herbert Goodland, deputy to Ellissen. Sir Fabian Ware was Master of the lodge in 1930 and the lodge jewel depicts, in coloured enamel, a Commission cemetery. In 1960, the organisation was renamed the Commonwealth War Graves Commission.

On 27 June 1919, an Especial Grand Lodge was held at the Royal Albert Hall to celebrate the peace. A message was read from the Grand Master, the Duke of Connaught:

> … to create a perpetual Memorial of its [i.e. the Craft's] gratitude to Almighty God…[to] render fitting honour to the many Brethren who fell during the War. I desire that the question of the Memorial be taken into early consideration… The great and continued growth of Freemasonry amongst us demands a central home; and I wish it to be considered whether the question

LEFT Past Master's jewel of Builders of the Silent Cities No. 4948 belonging to Henry Cart de Lafontaine.

RIGHT Four examples of the Hall Stone Jewel.

of erecting that home in this Metropolis of the Empire, dedicated to the Most High… would not be the most fitting Memorial.

In January 1920, details of an appeal to raise £1,000,000, to be called the Masonic Million Memorial Fund, were distributed to lodges and individual members. Contributions to the fund were to be marked by the award of medals. Individual members who contributed at least 10 guineas (£10.50) were to receive a silver medal and those who contributed 100 guineas (£105) or more, a gold medal. Lodges that contributed an average of 10 guineas per member were to have their names recorded in the new building as Hall Stone Lodges and the Master of each such lodge would be entitled to wear a special medal as a collarette. By the end of the appeal, 53,224 individual medals had been issued and 1,321 lodges had qualified as Hall Stone Lodges.

The running of the Fund became an enormous task and involved large amounts of paperwork, including individual record cards logging the amount and timing of each member's donation (which could be made over a period of years), handled by the Grand Secretary's office.

A design by H.V. Ashley and F. Winton Newman was chosen with building work beginning in 1927. The new Peace Memorial Building was dedicated on 19 July 1933. The theme of the memorial window in the vestibule area outside the Grand Temple was the attainment of peace through sacrifice. Its main feature was the Angel of Peace holding a model of the tower façade of the building. In the lower panels were shown fighting men, civilians and pilgrims ascending a winding staircase towards the Angel.

In June 1938, five years later, the Building Committee in its last report announced that it had given instructions for a memorial Shrine and Roll of Honour to be placed under the memorial window; at the Grand Lodge meeting on 5 June 1940, by which time the country was again at war, it was able to announce that the work had been completed. The memorial Shrine was designed by Walter Gilbert (1871-1946). In bronze, its design and ornamentation incorporated symbols connected with the theme of peace and the attainment of eternal life. It took the form of a bronze casket resting on an ark amongst reeds, indicative of a journey which had come to an end. In the centre of the front panel, a relief showed the Hand of God set in a circle in which rested the

BELOW Masonic Million Memorial Fund individual record cards for General Sir Reginald Wingate, the industrialist Sir John Brunner and the Masonic historian Douglas Knoop.

Soul of Man. At the four corners of the Shrine stood pairs of winged Seraphim carrying golden trumpets and across the front were four gilded figures portraying Moses, Joshua, Solomon and St George.

The Roll of Honour was guarded by kneeling figures representing the four fighting services (Royal Navy, Royal Marines, Army and Royal Flying Corps). On either side of the Shrine were bronze pillars of light decorated with wheat (for resurrection), lotus (for the waters of life) and irises (for eternal life) with four panels of oak leaves at their base. The Roll of Honour displayed at the Shrine on a parchment roll included over 350 names not included in the corresponding book and additional lodge details for about 30 names already known.

Across the country, Masonic provinces and lodges created their own memorials. One of the earliest was a memorial stone erected by members of Samson Lodge No. 1668 at the entrance to the Bayswater Synagogue in May 1916, marking the death of Lieutenant Victor Baron Barnett in France in 1915. The white Carrara stone contained a piece of Barnett's helmet and his uniform buttons.

THIS STONE WAS LAID BY
FIELD-MARSHAL H.R.H. THE
DUKE OF CONNAUGHT K.G.
M.W. GRAND MASTER
ON JULY 14 1927

TOP LEFT The foundation stone of the Masonic Peace Memorial building.

BOTTOM LEFT The bronze shrine containing the Roll of Honour parchment scroll.

RIGHT Founder's jewel for Memory Lodge No. 4264.

The Lodge of Verity No. 2739 commemorated lost members in an illuminated memorial book. The members of lodges in the province of Leicestershire decided a memorial should take two forms: a financial contribution of £5,000 towards the building of a new orthopaedic department at the Leicester Royal Infirmary and a memorial tablet at the Freemasons' Hall in Leicester. The four lodges in Scarborough provided X-ray equipment to Scarborough hospital in 1923 as a form of war memorial.

Epworth Lodge No. 3789, formed in 1917 for ministers and laymen associated with the Methodist Church, raised £300 for a memorial window in Wesley's Chapel, City Road in London, dedicated to all Methodists in the British Empire who had died in the war. The window was designed by Frank Salisbury and unveiled in May 1919 by Sir Horace Brooks Marshall, the Lord Mayor of London. A set of 12 stained glass panels were donated as a memorial to St Cuthbert's Church in north London by the members of Bowes Park Lodge No. 3119, in 1919. The panels were removed in the mid-1990s and eventually mounted within the Weymouth Masonic Temple in Dorset.

Amongst the many memorial plaques was a stone screen at Sherborne Abbey in Dorset, inscribed with the names of the Dorset brethren who died in the war. The memorial plaque at the Masonic Hall in Hope Street, Liverpool was flanked by wreathed armorial bearings on each side. One represented the arms of the United Grand Lodge of England, the other the Liver Bird bearing an olive branch.

In Brighton, Sussex, a senior Freemason within the province, William Porter, undertook to pay for the building of the Masonic Hall in Queen Street as a memorial to his only son, killed in the war, and provided £10,000 towards the cost. The building was finally opened in 1928. In Manchester, a decision had been made before the war to build a new hall on the site of the Queen's Theatre in Bridge Street. The building was dedicated by the Prince of Wales in 1929, when he unveiled the commemorative tablet on the west wall of the central Memorial Hall, enshrining 'the memory of all Freemasons from the province of East Lancashire who, of their Faith and Valour, made the Supreme Sacrifice for King and Country'. Another Peace Memorial was built in Broad Street, Birmingham designed by local Warwickshire architect and Freemason Rupert Savage. It opened in 1927.

Rifleman Harry Charles Carter was a member of St Mark's Lodge No. 2423. Married with a young son, he was captain of his local Church Lad's Brigade in Connah's Quay, North Wales, where he had worked before the war as an engineering draughtsman at the Sandycroft Foundry and Engineering Company. He became a stretcher bearer and was killed at the Somme in July 1916. His lodge wanted to establish a memorial and petitioned for a new lodge to be named after him. Grand Lodge was reluctant to allow this but did agree to the formation of Memory Lodge No. 4264 in 1921, dedicated to his memory. The lodge's jewel depicts a war memorial, the initials H.C., and the words 'He did his duty.'

ABOVE Memorial window at Freemasons' Hall, London.

'A PERMANENT MEMORIAL'

ABOVE The illuminated memorial of the Lodge of Verity No. 2739.

4

PRISONERS OF WAR

An estimated 190,000 British and Empire soldiers were captured and held as prisoners during World War One. Both sides also established internment camps to hold enemy aliens – civilians who were believed to be a potential threat and to sympathise with the enemy's war objectives. It is inevitable given the number of captives involved that a number of them were Freemasons and there is evidence of Masonic activities amongst both prisoners of war and internees.

Germany

Although there is no evidence of any formal Masonic meetings held by prisoners of war in German hands, it seems that Freemasons were able to identify each other, hold social gatherings and provide fraternal support for fellow Masons. There are cases of informal Masonic gatherings in both civilian and military internment camps.

When the war broke out in 1914, over 10,000 British nationals were living, working or on holiday in Germany. On 6 November 1914, the German government introduced internment for all enemy alien males aged between 17 and 55 years. Many of those interned were taken to Ruhleben internment camp at Spandau, west of Berlin. The camp was situated on a racecourse and barracks were built in and around the stables to house the 4-5,000 British and Empire civilians interned there for the duration of the war. The camp was run internally by the inmates, who quickly established a church, sports and social clubs, library, postal service and camp magazine.

On 18 December 1914, an address reached the Grand Secretary which had been sent from Ruhleben on 9 December. It began:

> We, the undersigned brethren, at present interned with other British civilians at the concentration camp at Ruhleben, Spandau, Germany, send hearty good wishes to the Grand Master, officers and brethren in Great Britain, hoping that we may have the pleasure soon of greeting them personally.

The letter was written by Walter P. Goodale of Freedom Lodge, No. 77, Gravesend, and accompanied a list over a hundred Freemasons. On 13 February 1915, Goodale sent another letter with a list of 45 other Freemasons, not included on the first list because they had either not yet arrived at the camp or had not then identified themselves. The two lists contained the names of Freemasons who were members of lodges in England and also in Australia, Egypt, Hong Kong, Ireland, Scotland, South Africa, South America, the United States, the West Indies and even Germany.

One notable Freemason who did not appear on either list was Captain Charles Fryatt of Star in the East Lodge, No. 650, Harwich. As a Merchant Navy captain, Fryatt was briefly sent to Ruhleben in 1916 after his ferry, S.S. *Brussels* was captured by German destroyers on 25 June. Fryatt had successfully defended two of his ships from German U-boat attacks a year earlier in March 1915, on the second occasion attempting to ram a submarine to stop it firing a torpedo. He had been rewarded for his actions with gold watches from both his employers, the Great Eastern Railway Company and the Admiralty. The latter watch was inscribed: 'Presented by the Lords Commissioners of the Admiralty to Chas. Algernon Fryatt Master of the S.S. *Brussels* in recognition of the example set by that vessel when attacked by a German submarine on March 28th, 1915.'

This inscription was used as an excuse by the German authorities to try Fryatt at a court martial and subsequently execute him. Fryatt's name is included on the Masonic Roll of Honour; it is also included as one of three names on a ceramic plaque erected in one of the wards of the Masonic Hospital shortly after the war, marking a donation by the Ruhleben internees. The other two names were Edward Russell and Alexander Cordiner; both were merchant seamen on ships located in German waters at the outbreak of the war. Russell was a member of the Earl of Yarborough Lodge No. 2770 in Grimsby and died of natural causes in the camp in December 1917. Cordiner was a member of St Hilda's Lodge No. 240 in South Shields; he died in March 1918.

On the whole, the civilian prisoners at Ruhleben were treated better than their military counterparts, the only real hardship being loss of freedom and food shortages. In August 1915 another of the internees, Percy Hull, wrote to Grand Lodge to advise that there were now about 200 Freemasons there, the majority receiving few, if any, food parcels. His letter helped to launch a well-publicised campaign to support the internees. The Board of General Purposes issued an appeal to lodges on behalf of brethren interned in enemy countries as civilian prisoners of war, in particular at Ruhleben. While regretting that it was financially prohibitive to send parcels to all Masonic prisoners of war, Alfred Robbins, welcomed the formation of what became known as the Ruhleben Fund:

> They are prisoners of war only in the sense of being detained during war time; and their case is particularly hard because their businesses have been ruined and they and their families brought near to destitution.

The fund enabled regular parcels to be sent to each Masonic internee. Grand Lodge approached Sir Richard Burbidge, the Managing Director of Harrods, Knightsbridge, for assistance and parcels were sent, most likely described as a 'Box of Good Cheer' containing biscuits, corned beef, cocoa, cigarettes and other commodities. One internee, S.F. Sheasby, a former pupil of the boys' school, reported in 1917 how welcome the parcels were, containing tea, coffee, cake, biscuits, potted meat and Quaker Oats. Percy Hull maintained careful records of those members entitled to receive parcels to ensure fairness; those prisoners repatriated from Ruhleben under an exchange system informed Grand Lodge that, without such assistance, their situation would have been much worse.

In 1917, Percy Hull organised the Freemasons in the camp to send fraternal greetings to the Grand Master on the bi-centenary of the formation of Grand Lodge. This was one of Hull's last acts as an inmate of Ruhleben, as he was then transferred to The Hague in the Netherlands. Just before he left Ruhleben, the

PRISONERS OF WAR

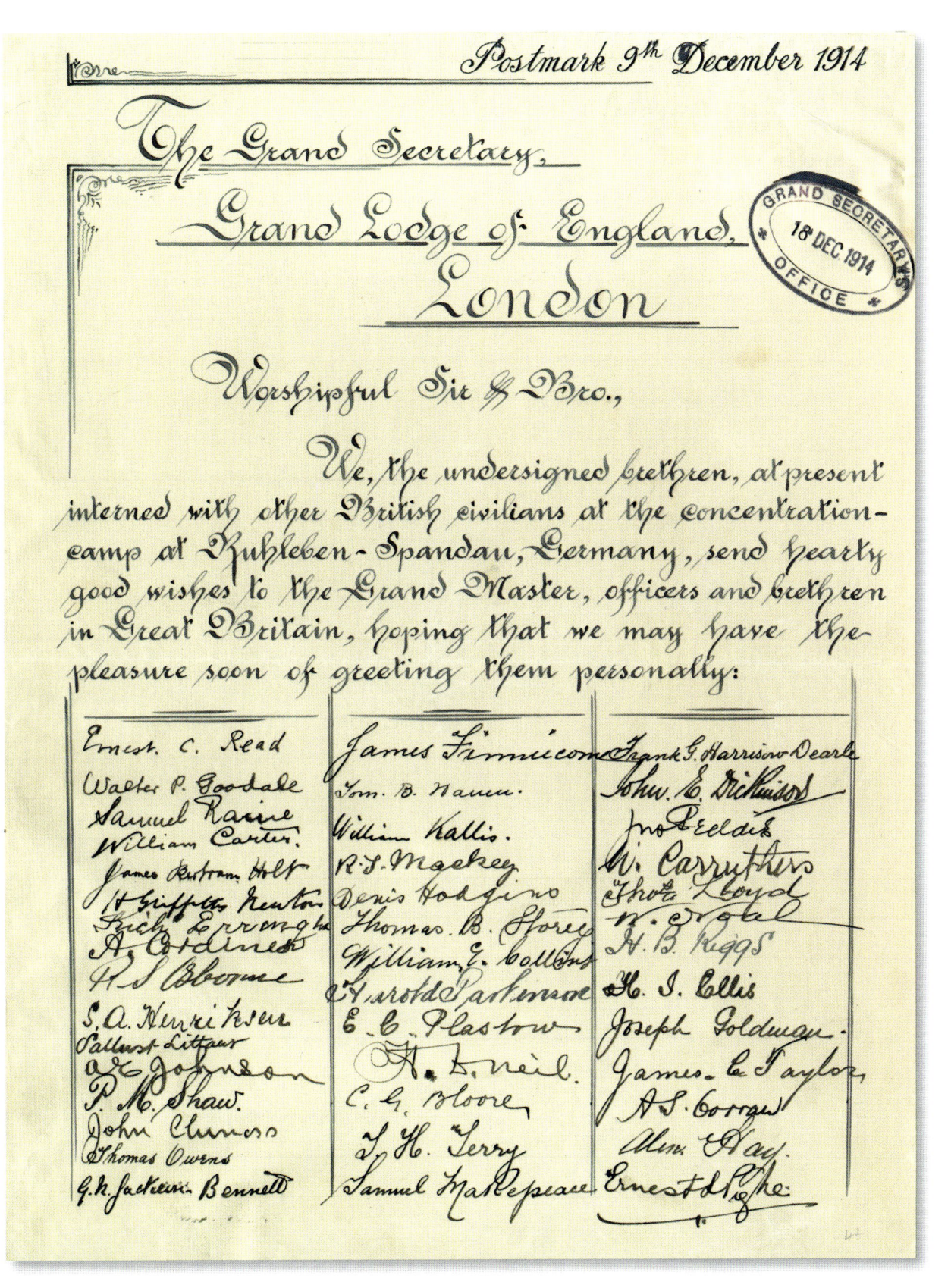

> Postmark 9th December 1914
>
> The Grand Secretary,
> Grand Lodge of England,
> London
>
> *GRAND SECRETARY'S OFFICE 18 DEC 1914*
>
> Worshipful Sir & Bro.,
>
> We, the undersigned brethren, at present interned with other British civilians at the concentration-camp at Ruhleben-Spandau, Germany, send hearty good wishes to the Grand Master, officers and brethren in Great Britain, hoping that we may have the pleasure soon of greeting them personally:

Ernest C. Read
Walter P. Goodale
Samuel Racine
William Carter
James Bertram Holt
H. Griffiths Newton
Ricky Errongton
A. Gardiner
R. S. Osborne
S. A. Henriksen
Sallust Litteur
A. E. Johnson
P. M. Shaw
John Chivers
Thomas Owens
G. K. Jackson Bennett

James Finnicom
Tom B. Nauen
William Kallis
R. J. Mackey
Denis Hodgins
Thomas B. Storey
William E. Collins
Harold Parkinson
E. C. Plastow
H. D. Neil
C. G. Bloore
L. H. Terry
Samuel Makepeace

Frank G. Harrison Dearle
John E. Dickinson
Jno. Eeldie
W. Carruthers
Thos. Lloyd
W. Orgal
H. B. Riggs
H. J. Ellis
Joseph Goldman
James E. Taylor
A. S. Corgen
Alex. Hay
Ernest L. Pyke

ABOVE Part of the letter sent by prisoners at Ruhleben to the Grand Secretary in 1914.

other Masonic inmates of the camp presented him with a loyal address thanking him for his support.

Just as Freemasons in the civilian internment camp at Ruhleben were able to seek each other out, so were Freemasons in military prisoner of war camps in Germany. Amongst a box of papers and letters relating to prisoners of war in the Library and Museum of Freemasonry, London, is an unpublished paper by Canadian Freemason Robert James Meekren (1876-1963) called *Masonic Experiences as a Prisoner of War*. Meekren was a member of the Grand Lodge of Quebec who would eventually become known to Freemasons for his articles in the American Masonic periodicals *American Tyler-Keystone* and *The Builder*, and for his membership of the English research lodge Quatuor Coronati No. 2076. He enlisted as a private in the University Company of Princess Patricia's Canadian Light Infantry and was sent overseas in 1915. He was wounded at Ypres on 2 June 1916 and taken prisoner. After several months recovering in hospital, Meekren was sent to Stenda Mannschaftslager Camp in Lower Saxony, a camp housing about 4,000 men, the majority of whom were Russian with about 1,500 Frenchmen and 200 from the British Empire.

Meekren was keen to discover if any of his fellow prisoners were Freemasons. When directly asking people proved unfruitful, he resorted to embroidering a blue silk square and compasses onto his tunic.

> This was effective and a few days afterwards a Sergeant Major of one of the Highland Regiments came up to me and asked if I had ever been entirely destitute. I said that I had and as a matter of fact was entirely destitute at that particular moment. However it dawned on me what he was referring to and I found that he was a member of a lodge in Scotland.

The Scotsman introduced Meekren to other Freemasons, including two Frenchmen, one of whom

LEFT Jewel for Star in the East Lodge No. 650.

RIGHT Ceramic plaque installed at the Royal Masonic Hospital.

gave him 100 German Marks, underclothes and clean shirts. He soon discovered that the French Freemasons were very efficient at seeking out their international brethren.

> It was Bro. Levy's habit when a party of new prisoners came into the camp to get hold of one or two of the other Masons and with them to take steps to discover if any of the newcomers belonged to the Craft; if they did he immediately took steps to do what was possible for their assistance.

It is notable that issues such as Grand Lodge affiliation, at a time when the English and French Grand Lodges had no formal communication, played no part in this Masonic support.

Meekren does not describe any formal Masonic activities such as lodge meetings or lodges of instruction. His paper mainly describes the charitable and social aspects of Freemasonry, such as a St. John's Day feast organised by the French brethren at the camp in the summer of 1917.

In the summer of 1917 as St. John's Day drew near, the French brethren proposed that we have

> THE EQUIPMENT OF THIS WARD WAS PRESENTED BY THE BRITISH FREEMASONS WHO WERE INTERNED IN RUHLEBEN, GERMANY, DURING THE GREAT WAR, 1914 TO 1918, AS A TOKEN OF THEIR DEEP GRATITUDE TO THE CRAFT FOR THE FRATERNAL HELP AND RELIEF EXTENDED TO THEM DURING THAT PERIOD OF CAPTIVITY AND DISTRESS: AND IN MEMORY OF THEIR FELLOW PRISONERS,
> BRO. CAPTAIN C. FRYATT, S.S. "BRUSSELS",
> BRO. CAPTAIN E. RUSSELL, S.S. "BURY",
> BRO. CAPTAIN A. CORDINER, S.S. "HEWORTH",
> TO WHOM DEATH BROUGHT RELEASE.
>
> PERCY C. HULL, P.D.G.O. ENG.

a little feast at which all the Masons in the camp should be present…We spoke three different languages, unless one could count broad Scots as a fourth. We drank coffee and French chocolate, and had a miscellaneous assortment of foods from bully beef to canned French chicken. Afterwards we smoked German cigars and drank toasts of chocolate and coffee and made speeches… It was the last chance that most of us had of meeting for very shortly afterwards most of the French brethren were sent away to other camps and I have no idea what became of them.

Prisoners of war were able to receive post from home and Meekren was regularly sent lodge summonses from his Canadian lodge, Golden Rule No. 5 in Stanstead, Quebec, letting him know what was happening in their meetings. These summonses were read by a German censor called Putz, who then identified himself to Meekren as a Freemason. Putz showed Meekren a good deal of fraternal kindness throughout his captivity. All prisoners who were not commissioned officers were required to report for physical labour; Putz knew that Meekren was suffering because of his injuries and arranged a clerical job for him. He also warned Meekren when letters from an English friend contained comments about the progress of the war. This could have earned Meekren time in solitary confinement but, because of Putz's intervention, he was able to ask his friend not to write again. Private Meekren's membership of the Craft certainly helped him through some difficult times during his period of captivity. After the war, he remained an active and enthusiastic Freemason until his death at the age of 87 in 1963.

LEFT Half-penny in case, sold at the 1915 Installation of Duke of Edinburgh Lodge No. 1529 in aid of Freemasons interned overseas.

RIGHT Details of Harrods' parcels for men on active service and prisoners.

Switzerland

Under the auspices of the International Committee of the Red Cross in 1914, the governments of Switzerland, Germany, France, Britain, Russia and Belgium agreed that captured military and naval personnel who were too sick or seriously wounded to continue in military service could be repatriated through Switzerland with the assistance of the Swiss Red Cross. This was expanded to include others who were sick or badly wounded but who might return to military service if repatriated, all of whom were to be interned in Switzerland to aid their recovery. During the course of the war nearly 68,000 men from all countries were interned there.

The first British former prisoners of war arrived in Switzerland in May 1916. They were held in two camps at Mürren and Châteux d'Oex in the southwest of the country. The locations were not ideal to aid recovery as Mürren was built on a ledge high up on a mountain and often cut off in the winter. If their wounds or illnesses permitted, internees were expected to work but otherwise there was little to do.

Henry Billinghurst, Past Provincial Grand Warden for Essex and a manager at piano manufacturers John Brinsmead & Sons Ltd in Wigmore Street, London, helped to establish the British Interned Prisoners in Switzerland Fund. He set up a technical training scheme under the auspices of the British Red Cross at both the Mürren and Château d'Oex camps, and organised, financed and sent volunteer instructors to run classes in carpentry, joinery, cabinet making, French polishing and piano making. Sir Arthur Stanley endorsed the work undertaken by Billinghurst, stating in December 1917: 'the scheme as put forward by you and adopted by us was much the most practical thing that has been done in connection with the training of these men, who owe a great debt of gratitude to you and your firm.'

The Netherlands

On 14 October 1914, the city of Antwerp fell to the Germans after a short siege. The First Royal Naval Brigade, an infantry regiment trying to make a break to Ostend, under Commodore Wilfred Henderson, was forced to escape into the Netherlands to avoid capture by the enemy. As the Netherlands was a neutral country, under international conventions, Henderson and his brigade of 1,500 men were interned there for the remainder of the war.

The Brigade were taken to barracks just outside the town of Groningen and set to work building their own accommodation. The camp, which was built

Acceptable Gifts for the Man on Service.

No. 1.
HARRODS
5/- Box of Good Cheer
For despatch to
Prisoners of War in Germany.

CONTENTS:
1 tin of Biscuits.
1 box Wheatmeal Rations.
1 pkt. Muscatels.
1 ,, Bivouac Cocoa and Milk.
1 tin Corned Beef.
1 ,, Christmas Pudding.
1 pkt. Chocolate.
2 pkts. Glass Lemon.

The above will be sent to Prisoners of War for
FIVE SHILLINGS.

No. 2.
— HARRODS —
Half-Guinea Box
For the Dardanelles

CONTENTS:
1 tin Chocolate
1 ,, Christmas Pudding
1 ,, Meat Lozenges
1 ,, Apricots
1 ,, Acid Sweets
1 box 50 Virginia Cigarettes
1 tube Insect Ointment
1 Maxem Belt, a preventative against vermin of all kinds

THE ABOVE SENT POST FREE FOR
10/6
TO THE DARDANELLES.

---

almost entirely of wood, had a schoolroom, a Mission for Seamen church, rooms for a camp newsletter and magazine, a shed for the drama group, sports pitches and a parade ground. The camp was called Timbertown by the British and *Het Engelse Kamp* 'the English Camp' by the Groningen residents.

Unlike prisoners of war in Germany, the inmates of Groningen had a fair amount of freedom. They were allowed into the local town, initially with guards but later on their own. The camp ran several sports clubs which competed with local teams. The Brigade's band regularly paraded through the town and the local people were able to enjoy orchestra concerts and performances by the camp's music and drama club, 'the Timbertown Follies'.

On 9 March 1915, Commodore Henderson, who was a member of Navy Lodge No. 2612, London, wrote to the Master of Loge L'Union Provinçiale, Groningen and asked if the brethren of the Groningen lodge would allow British Freemasons interned locally to use their Temple if they were given permission to start their own lodge. Several members of the camp who were Freemasons had already visited the lodge but found the ceremonies very difficult to follow in Dutch. Henderson then wrote to the United Grand Lodge of England, who replied that he and his fellow interned brethren should apply to the Grand Orient of the Netherlands for a warrant to start a new lodge as it was under that Grand Lodge's Masonic jurisdiction. This was duly achieved with the new lodge called *Gastvrijheid Loge* meaning 'Hospitality Lodge' and numbered 113.

The new lodge was consecrated on 22 May 1915 and Commodore Henderson was installed as the first Master. Loge L'Union Provinciale presented Gastvrijheid Lodge with a presentation gavel and the wands of the lodge officers. In the next 3 and a half years, the lodge met 55 times and initiated 64

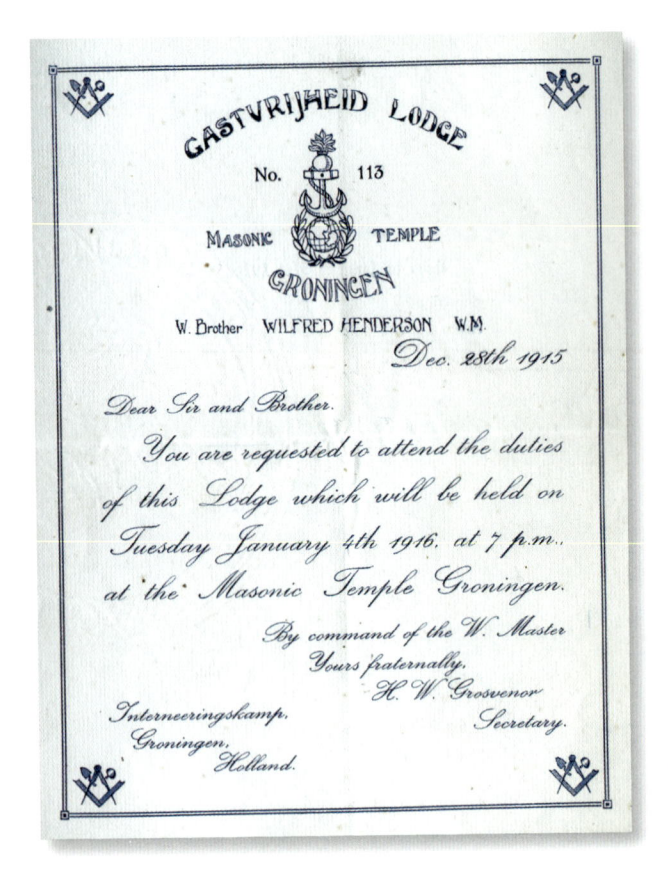

ABOVE Summons for Gastvrijheid Lodge No. 113, December 1915.

internees into Freemasonry before relocating to London at the end of the war. The lodge minutes, which still survive, show that these three years were not without some memorable incidents.

The Grand Orient of the Netherlands treated the lodge just like any other and its Masters and Wardens were summoned to attend meetings of the Grand Orient in The Hague which because of the nature of their internment they were allowed to do. Camp internees could even travel much further than the Netherlands if they were granted parole and promised to return. Commodore Henderson translated the Grand Orient's *Constitutions* into English and, in 1917, arranged for 100 copies to be printed in the camp. He personally delivered a copy of the book to Freemasons' Hall in London later that year, granted parole because his daughter had been involved in a riding accident. By January 1918, Henderson was back in Groningen and, at a meeting of Gastvrijheid Lodge on 29 January, gave an account to the members of all the London lodges he had visited during his short stay in England.

Henderson recognised that the lodge was a valuable asset in the smooth running of the internment camp. It was good for the morale of the members of the lodge, giving them a regular activity to look forward to; it was also good for the relationship with the local population and for the discipline of the interned men, for all members of the lodge were expected to show good, moral behaviour.

In September 1916, the lodge voted to exclude Petty Officer Albert Shute from the lodge after he was found to have fathered a child with a local woman, whom he had set up in a house in Amsterdam, despite having a wife back in England. Commodore Henderson believed the affair could have had serious implications both for the camp and the lodge as everyone in Groningen knew about it. Although he recommended that Shute was excluded from the lodge, he decided not to ask the Grand Orient to expel Shute from Freemasonry, in case he mended his ways in later life and wanted to return to the Craft.

Albert Shute's exclusion was the exception because the lodge continued to grow as the war progressed. By the end of 1916, there were sufficient numbers to contemplate working the additional degrees of Freemasonry. On 11 November 1916, Gastvrijheid Rose Croix Chapter was formed by the Supreme Council of the Netherlands to work the degrees of the Ancient and Accepted Scottish Rite.

On 6 July 1918, a second lodge for British Prisoners of War was established in the Netherlands, after military and civilian prisoners who had been in German camps for 18 months or more began to be transferred to neutral countries. Its founding Master was an army officer, Lieutenant Colonel J.A.C. Gibbs, and the new lodge was called Willem van Oranje Lodge No. 118.

Willem van Oranje Lodge was consecrated by Dr M.S. Lingbeck, the Grand Master of the Grand Orient of the Netherlands. The founders of the lodge all wore aprons that had been made and sent to Holland by Miss Marie Randall, the sister of the Senior Deacon, Captain Henry Randall. Their working tools were made by Freemasons from Gastvrijheid Lodge; Baron van Ittersum presented the lodge with an ebony gavel and one of the founders, Captain M.G. Sandemann, painted the lodge's tracing boards.

The lodge had lost their first Master by August 1918 because Gibbs had been repatriated due to ill health. While in England, he met the Grand Secretary and tried to solve a dilemma facing the lodge. In a letter dated 26 September he wrote:

> I meant to have put a conundrum to you the other day but forgot. A man who was in Ruhleben, asked to join the Willem v. Oranje – although English he had only done Masonry in a Hun Lodge. This I did not feel inclined to grant, owing to the circumstances of all intercourse between the G.L. of England & Germany being off… I suggested he put his case on paper to me & got Hull to verify the facts.

The 'Hull' mentioned was Percy Hull, the organist who had been interned at Ruhleben internment camp since the outbreak of the war, and the member of the German lodge was an Englishman called Fran Harrison-Dearle, a resident of Bremen since 1907. Harrison-Dearle had signed the loyal address to Hull in 1917 when he left Ruhleben and was one of the Ruhleben Freemasons who wrote to Grand Lodge in 1914. He explained that he had resigned from his German lodge when war was declared and had not had any contact with German Freemasons apart from two other Ruhleben internees. The Grand Secretary's answer to this dilemma is not recorded. It would have been interesting to note what it was as, although the United Grand Lodge of England had broken off relations with its German counterparts, Willem van Oranje was affiliated to the Grand Orient of the Netherlands which had not.

On 11 November 1918, the armistice was signed and the war in Europe came to an end. Both Dutch lodges had already been preparing to return to England. Many of the original officers of Willem van Oranje returned before the armistice through ill health and Gastvrijheid was able to send its officers to fill in. Baron van Ittersum presented Commodore Henderson with an ancient 18th-Century Dutch poignard to pass onto Gastvrijheid Lodge at their last meeting on 5 November 1918. Willem van Oranje Lodge was due to hold its final meeting on 21 November 1918. They even had a summons printed with details of 12 men who were to be balloted for initiation, including Sergeant Stanley H. Sawyer of the Lancashire Fusiliers. However, the meeting did not take place as, by then, most of the lodge members were on their way home. Sergeant Sawyer was finally initiated in London on 29 November 1919, in what was now Willem Van Oranje Lodge No. 3976. Gastvrijheid was also transferred to London and, on 7 April 1919, became Gastvrijheid Lodge No. 3970, for members of the Royal Naval Volunteer Reserve. Willem Van Oranje Lodge's new by-laws stated that they were now a lodge for all former Prisoners of War, military and civilian.

Turkey

The Ottoman Empire treated prisoners of war poorly compared with the other Central Powers. After the fall of Kut in Mesopotamia, on 29 April 1916, the 10,000 British Empire soldiers who surrendered were forcibly marched over 1,000 kilometres to camps in central Turkey, with nearly 4,000 dying on route. Many were already in poor health after a five-month siege. About 100 officers and 60 orderlies were sent to the town of Yozgad in the Anatolia region. A camp was set up in six large houses on the edge of town that had once belonged to wealthy local Armenians. The camp was unusual in that it did not have many fences, just the walled gardens of the houses, and very few guards. What kept the prisoners in place were the miles of wilderness around Yozgad and the bandits who inhabited it.

In 1917, Major Ernest George Dunn of the Royal Ulster Rifles wrote to the United Grand Lodge of England asking if there was any possibility of obtaining a warrant for a lodge amongst the prisoners of war in Yozgad POW Camp. In the meantime, he was starting a Lodge of Instruction, called *Cappadocia*, with eight fellow Masons.

The minutes of Cappadocia Lodge of Instruction still exist. They were recorded in a small exercise book by the Secretary, Captain Roy T. Sweet, formerly a member of McMahon Lodge No. 3262 in Quetta like Major Dunn, with additions by Dunn himself. Just after the war, Dunn gave the minutes to his London lodge, the Lodge of Antiquity No. 2, who deposited them in the Library and Museum along with two aprons made from handkerchiefs and scraps purchased in the local market.

The minutes show that, as a Lodge of Instruction, Cappadocia was active from 14 February until 13 September 1918. A note from Dunn accompanying the book recorded that:

> We met surreptitiously every other Friday, first in a room which was used as a chapel and latterly in a store-room. One Brother, being charged to hang about unostentatiously outside, acted as 'outer guard' and only once was a meeting innocently disturbed by our captors who remained in ignorance, or apparent ignorance, to the end.

As Cappadocia was only a Lodge of Instruction they could not initiate new Masons, so their meetings were restricted to those members of the camp who were already Freemasons. Their meetings usually centred around practising the three Craft ceremonies, with the members taking it in turns to perform the roles of the lodge officers. Sometimes Dunn, who was an experienced Freemason, would give a lecture. The book contains a detailed transcript of a lecture on Masonic jewels that he gave on 12 April 1918, together with his colour illustrations, drawn from memory.

The meetings of the lodge were disrupted from time to time by events in and around the camp. The lodge's Inner Guard, Lieutenant Elias H. Jones, missed one of Dunn's lectures because, as the minutes record, he 'was undergoing confinement for being in telepathic communication with some person or persons unknown'. Jones' confinement was part of a bizarre but ultimately successful escape plan. He and an Australian called C.W. Hill had fooled the commandant and interpreter into believing that they were mediums, who could, through the guidance of a spirit, direct the commandant to riches left behind by the town's former Armenian population. Jones' and Hill's exploits eventually led to them faking insanity, being transferred to a mental hospital in Istanbul and eventually being repatriated to Britain. The full story of Jones' escape can be read in his own account, *The Road to En-Dor*, published in 1919.

Further disruption was caused after the meeting on 12 April, when the imminent departure of the Senior Warden, Junior Deacon and Treasurer and their transfer to a camp in Afion Karahissar was announced. The men had been moved with several other inmates to accommodate 44 officers and 25 men whom Jones called the 'Kastomou Incorrigibles', a group of prisoners who had refused to give their word not to escape after a mass break-out from Kastomou camp in 1917. However, there were Freemasons amongst the Kastomou Incorrigibles and the lodge gained three new members: Lieutenants Scaife, Sheridan and O'Donoghue.

PRISONERS OF WAR

ABOVE Photograph of members of Willem van Oranje Lodge No. 118 (NC) in military uniform.

LEFT Founder's jewel for Willem van Oranje Lodge No. 118 (NC).

Sheridan's attendance at the lodge was brief. On 30 August he was part of a mass break-out of 25 officers from the camp, although in the minutes of the final meeting on the 13 September, Sweet wrote, 'Major Dunn expressed the sympathies of the Lodge on the recapture of Bro. Lieut. Sheridan.'

It was here that the minutes end. Major Dunn wrote some notes explaining that, after the mass break-out, the Turks clamped down on the camp and they were all confined to barracks for the remainder of the war. He finished on a sad note:

> Before closing I wish to place on record the great regret we felt at the untimely death of Bro. Captain Sweet DSO after nearly two and a half years of captivity and only a few weeks before the armistice was signed. This gallant Brother fell a victim to the epidemic of influenza which swept the camp in October 1918.

Great Britain

At the outbreak of war, there were over 70,000 Germans and Austrians living and working in Britain. Like their British counterparts in Germany, men of fighting age were interned for the duration of the war. Many of the interned Germans were members of English, Scottish or Irish lodges, including the two German-speaking lodges that met under the United Grand Lodge in London; Pilgrim Lodge No. 238 and Deutschland Lodge No. 3315.

LEFT Apron of Captain John James Hughes, Australian Imperial Force and Willem van Oranje Lodge No. 118.

RIGHT Apron made out of handkerchiefs and used by members of the Cappadocia Lodge of Instruction.

Both the German speaking lodges were suspended in 1915, when the United Grand Lodge decreed that all enemy aliens could no longer attend meetings. The last annual membership return from Deutschland Lodge No. 3315, dated 30 March 1915, shows that the war had already had a serious effect on the lodge's membership with 17 of their 33 members resigning on 16 October 1914 because they had either been repatriated or interned.

In the archives of the United Grand Lodge of England there are several letters from inmates of British internment camps. On 22 January 1916 F.L. Schanfeld and Heinrich Wilhelm Blusch wrote to the Grand Secretary, Sir Edward Letchworth, from Camp Stobs near Hawick, asking for financial assistance for interned Freemasons' families and help in getting those over fighting age repatriated. They also said a lodge of instruction had been formed by 35 brethren in the camp whose ages ranged from 29 to 62.

A letter dated 13 March 1916 from Henry Junker of New Cross Lodge No. 1559, formerly the manager of the Charing Cross Hotel, and Carl Adolf Fuhr of Mount Lebanon Lodge No. 73, sent from the camp in the Cornwallis Road Workhouse in Islington, asked for permission to set up a lodge of instruction and sent a list of 13 brethren from English lodges who were fellow inmates.

Another letter, dated 3 April 1916, from Oskar Fritz of Cheerybles Lodge, No. 2466, London from Camp 3, Knockaloe, Isle of Man, asked for Grand

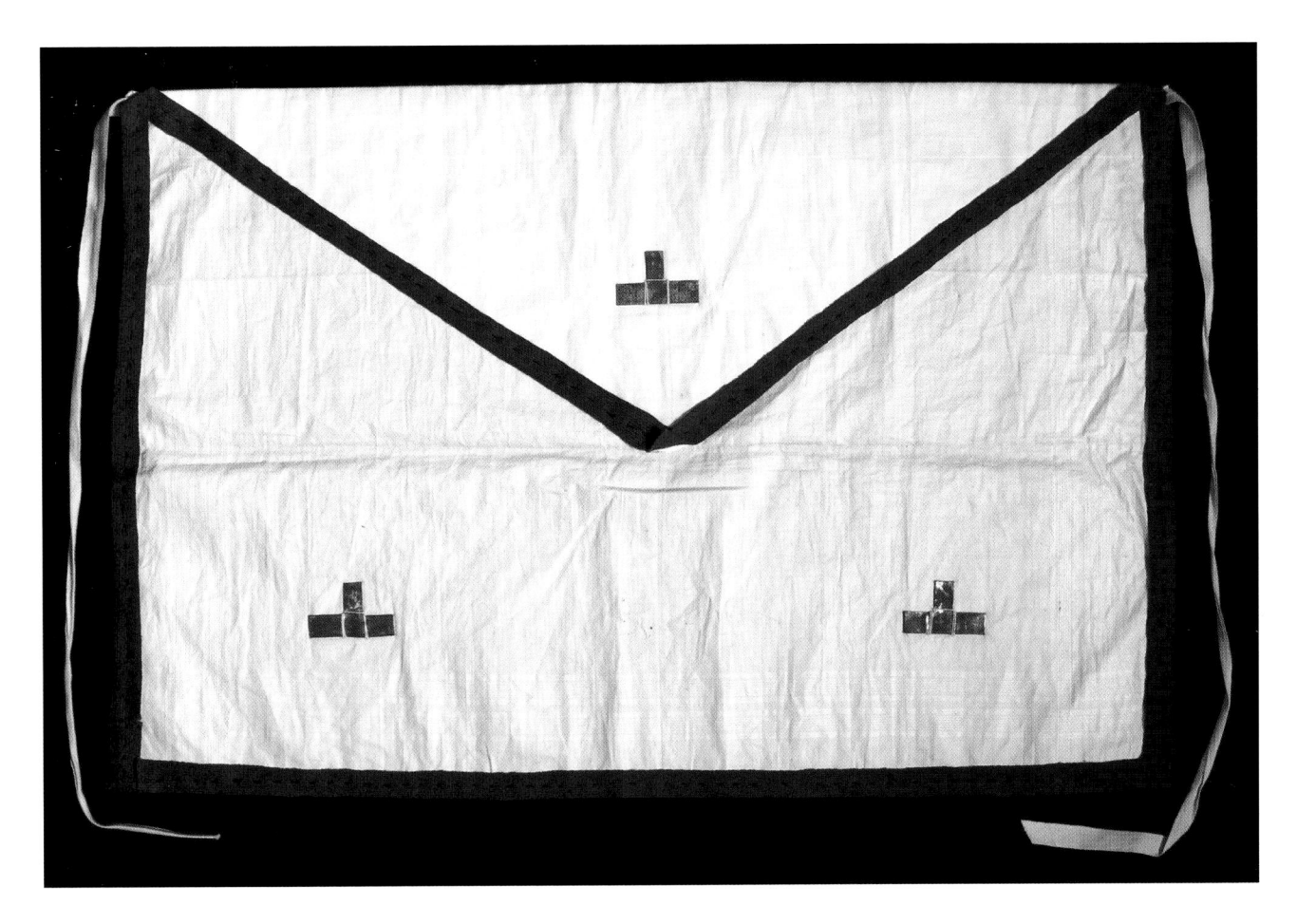

Lodge's assistance in getting permission to hold a regular meeting amongst the 50 or so Masons interned in all the Knockaloe camps, and also for permission to subscribe to Masonic journals such as *The Freemason*, *Freemasons' Chronicle*, *Hamburger Logenblatt* and *Der Ziekel*.

The Grand Secretary replied to all of them. In all his replies he was polite but firm, referring to his correspondent by their Masonic title. His answer to Brother Junker was typical:

> … having regard to the resolution of Grand Lodge passed on 1 August prohibiting members of the Craft of Alien birth from attending any Masonic meetings, they cannot advise the Grand Master to sanction the holding of a Lodge of Instruction in the Prisoner of War camp at Islington.

There is no record of what happened to the Lodges of Instruction that had already started or those that interned Masons wished to start. There would have been no reason why the men could not have held informal meetings like their Ruhleben counterparts. After the war, some of the internees sought to revive their membership. Carl Fuhr was finally readmitted to Mount Lebanon Lodge in January 1932.

It is a testament to the importance of Freemasonry in men's lives during the war that, even when they were unfortunate enough to be captured or interned, they still wanted to take part in Masonic activities. Whether it was to relieve the boredom of captivity or for some higher purpose, it appears that Freemasons were willing to go to great lengths to practise their Craft and bring others into the fraternity.

5

APRONS, ARMS AND ALMS: MASONIC CHARITY AND THE WAR

The message from the Masonic charities to lodge and chapter members in August 1914 was that it was 'business as usual'. From reading their formal transactions, at first glance it would appear that the Board of Benevolence, funded by annual contributions from lodges on the basis of the number of their subscribing members, and the Masonic charities, the Royal Masonic Institution for Girls (RMIG), the Royal Masonic Institution for Boys (RMIB) and the Royal Masonic Benevolent Institution (RMBI), continued to raise and distribute funds, without any significant alteration, for the duration of the war. However, careful examination of the formal record in conjunction with other resources, such as Masonic periodicals and publications issued by the schools, reveal details about the impact of hostilities on the Masonic charities, including the creation of new, war-related causes for which to raise funds and the tentative formation of what emerged post-war as the Royal Masonic Hospital. The RMIG had been formed in 1788. In 1914, its school to provide education for the daughters of deceased and distressed Freemasons was based at Clapham. The RMIB, dating from 1798, had maintained its own school since 1857, located since 1903 at Bushey in Hertfordshire. Both institutions also provided grants for the daughters and sons of Freemasons to be educated at other schools under a system called 'out education'. The RMBI had established an old people's home, the 'Asylum for Aged and Decayed Freemasons', at Croydon, in 1850. It also provided regular cash payments, known as annuities, to support elderly Freemasons.

All English Freemasons were encouraged 'to do their bit', whether joining the services or contributing financially to assist others affected by the war. While lodges might curtail entertainments and effect economies, it was understood that such measures were needed in order that 'their world-famed charities should not feel the pinch of changed conditions'. As the Reverend Henry Telford Hayman, Past Grand Chaplain and Deputy Provincial Grand Master of Nottinghamshire, went on to remind members when speaking in 1916, every Freemason joins because he wants to:

… help the broken hearted, the little orphan child, the widow, and the old man who has fallen by the way. We stand then for sympathy and self-sacrifice, to give ourselves for those who need our help.

A report by the Board of General Purposes in September 1914 suggested, 'Grand Lodge will wish to join in the great national movement for the relief of distress and alleviation of suffering, and proposals will be submitted to this end,' which led to generous Masonic contributions from members at home and abroad being directed to several non-Masonic causes. Lodges were encouraged to 'make such grants towards the Relief Funds as are within their power' while reassuring members that 'for those that fall in the struggle or who sustain severe loss, sincere sympathy will be extended and ready aid afforded within the agencies of which the Craft is possessed'. It had become common in the 1700s for charities to raise money at events such as concerts or dinners, which provided donors with entertainment and linked social activities with charitable aims. The Masonic charities used this festival system usually under the patronage of a Provincial Grand Master or other senior Freemason. In 1914, the Chairman of the RMIG Festival was the Grand Master, the Duke of Connaught, and the festival raised £27,492. The Chairman of the RMIB Festival which raised £37,043, was Sir Thomas Vansittart Bowater, the Lord Mayor of London. Income from donations, of which the festivals were a major element, represented about 70 percent of each charity's total income. There was concern about the impact of the war but it was decided that festivals would continue and, although receipts in 1915 were below those of the previous year, donations then increased substantially. The 1918 festivals raised more than £200,000 in total, an increase of 65 percent compared with the total raised in 1913.

All the charities made efficiencies or adopted novel income-raising objectives in an attempt to become more self-sufficient. By the summer of 1917, pupils at the Boys' School had dug beds for growing potatoes,

LEFT **The Royal Masonic Institution for Boys at Bushey.**

beetroot, carrots, artichokes, cauliflowers and beans. Although harvests were affected by wireworm, such crops helped to supplement the restricted wartime diet. By the autumn of 1917, they were collecting wood to heat school fires and, following an appeal from the Ministry of Munitions, also collecting bushels of acorns from which acetone was extracted to manufacture cordite for explosives. In 1918 girls at Clapham collected sphagnum moss, which was made into medical swabs at the local Red Cross depot.

At the outbreak of war, employment opportunities for single women as servants, secretaries and in other roles significantly declined as businesses closed down or reduced their activity. The Queen's Work for Women Fund was established. Grand Lodge requested Margaret, Lady Ampthill, the wife of the Pro Grand Master and a lady in waiting to Queen Mary, to form a ladies committee to raise contributions for this fund from the wives and daughters of Freemasons. £2,001 was raised and presented to Queen Mary at a reception at Buckingham Palace in March 1915. The funds raised were divided between several bodies providing training and other support for women, including the Professional Classes War Relief Council, the Association of Women Clerks and Secretaries Relief Fund and the Society of Women Journalists Relief Fund. However, as women began to replace

BELOW **Postcard image of the Royal Masonic Institution for Girls at Clapham.**

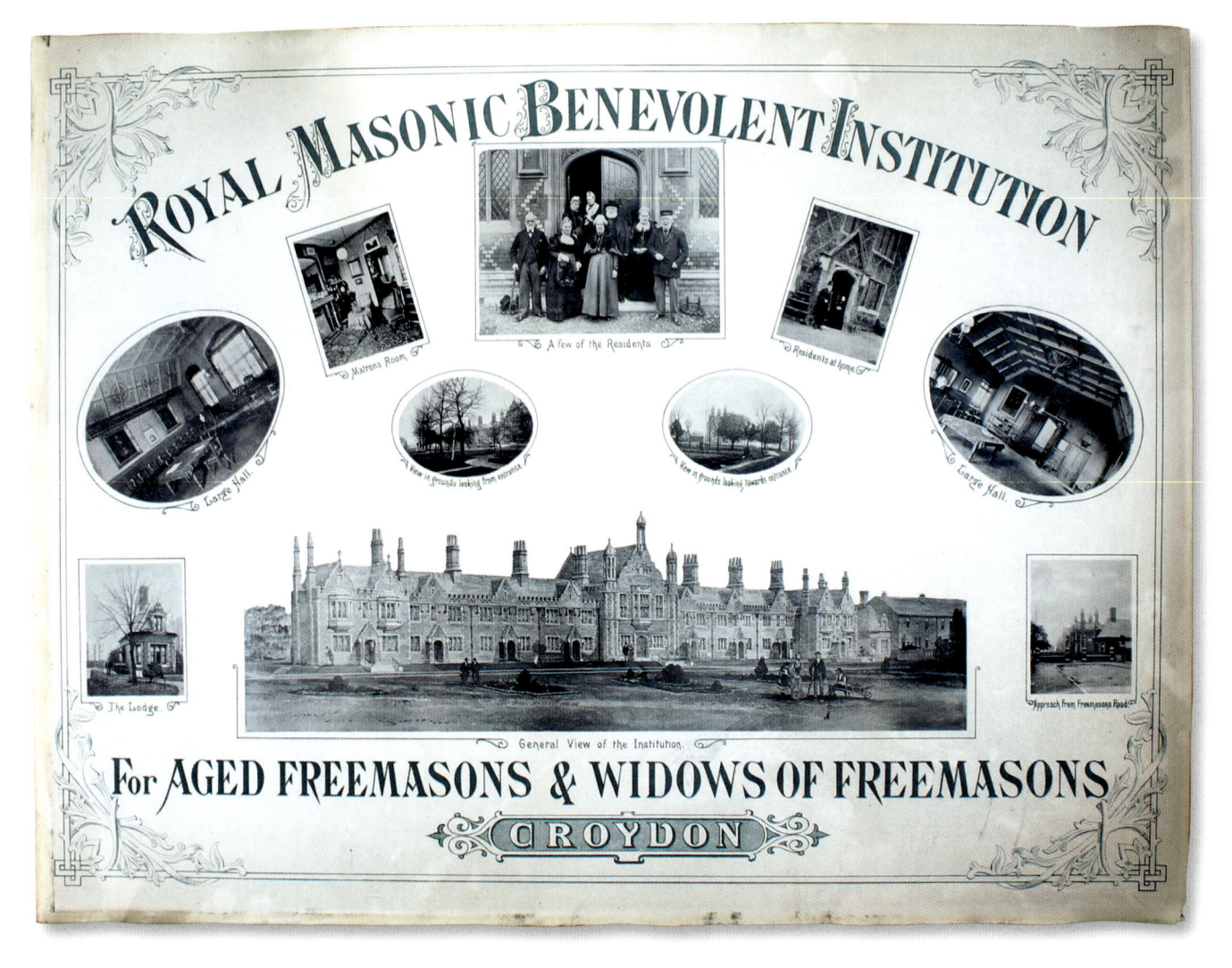

ABOVE The Asylum for Aged and Decayed Freemasons at Croydon.

men in clerical and manufacturing roles as the war continued, especially after the introduction of conscription in 1916, the Work for Women Fund was no longer required.

Other donations included support for the National Relief Fund, to which Grand Lodge contributed approximately £5,000, and the British Red Cross Society to which more than £2,000 was donated before March 1919, including a significant contribution of £500 from the District Grand Lodge of South America (Southern Division).

Established almost as soon as hostilities commenced, the relationship with the Red Cross was doubtless facilitated by Arthur Stanley, Provincial Grand Master of Lancashire, Western Division from 1910, who was appointed Chairman of the Executive Committee of the Red Cross in 1914. From December 1914 freemasons serving with the British Red Cross and St John's Ambulance Association were treated on a par with those on active service and not excluded for arrears of membership dues.

The Red Cross benefitted in other ways from Masonic support, with numerous former pupils of the Girls' School helping the charity. One Red Cross nurse, Mrs Agnes W. Brown née Stephenson, prepared her home at Bickley, Kent to receive 40 wounded soldiers, as well as assisting at a home for refugees.

Writing to the Girls' School magazine, *Massonica*, in January 1915, she remarked, 'I was very glad of my old Masonic training and discipline in the work of handling many people and getting ready' after being given only 24 hours' notice of the arrival of a party of Belgian refugees.

Former school nurse Mrs Effie R. Bellamy served as lady superintendent of a 50-bed Red Cross hospital at Sleaford, Lincolnshire, receiving a Royal Red Cross, Second Class medal in recognition of her war time efforts. Another former pupil, Emma Hardy, sent reports to *Massonica* about work as a Red Cross Voluntary Aid Detachment (VAD) nurse at Cardiff Infirmary and later 'somewhere in France' while May Pickles sent news about her work as a VAD at a military hospital at Salonika.

ABOVE Reverend Henry Telford Hayman.

LEFT RMBI Festival programme, 1918

According to news from former pupils sent to *The Masonian* in April 1916, C. Shipman of the Royal Navy Volunteer Reserve had been sent to Antwerp to help evacuate the remnants of the Belgian Army. On arrival he acted as an interpreter, 'thanks to the splendid tuition in French I received under Mr Roberts,' a teacher at the Boys' School. A former pupil at the Girls' School, Nurse Doris Sall, sent a report to *Massonica* about the arrival of Belgian soldiers, who arrived waving handkerchiefs and caps shouting, 'Old England for ever' and 'Long Live the King', on a ward staffed by French-speaking staff at

LEFT Jewels from festivals held between 1914 and 1918.

RIGHT Fundraising material for the Queen's Work for Women Fund.

BELOW Lady Ampthill.

Birmingham General Hospital in October 1914. One nurse thought she had asked a soldier to put his foot on the floor but, to his great amusement, said 'ceiling' instead!

Numerous refugees, assisted by the War Refugees Committee (WRC), began to arrive at Folkestone, Kent from Ostend. A public appeal to help was launched in the national press on 24 August 1914 and, within two weeks, the WRC was able to offer support to some 100,000 displaced persons. By mid-September, approximately 500 refugees were arriving daily in London, exacerbated by the fall of Antwerp and then Ostend. Following an immediate donation of £1,000 in September 1914, a further £2,000 raised by lodges and districts in England and overseas had been sent by Grand Lodge to various Belgian relief funds by 1918.

The loss of Lord Kitchener, Secretary of State for War and Past District Grand Master of Egypt and the Sudan, and many others, aboard HMS Hampshire in 1916 resonated with many members. Grand Lodge donated 250 guineas to the Lord Kitchener National

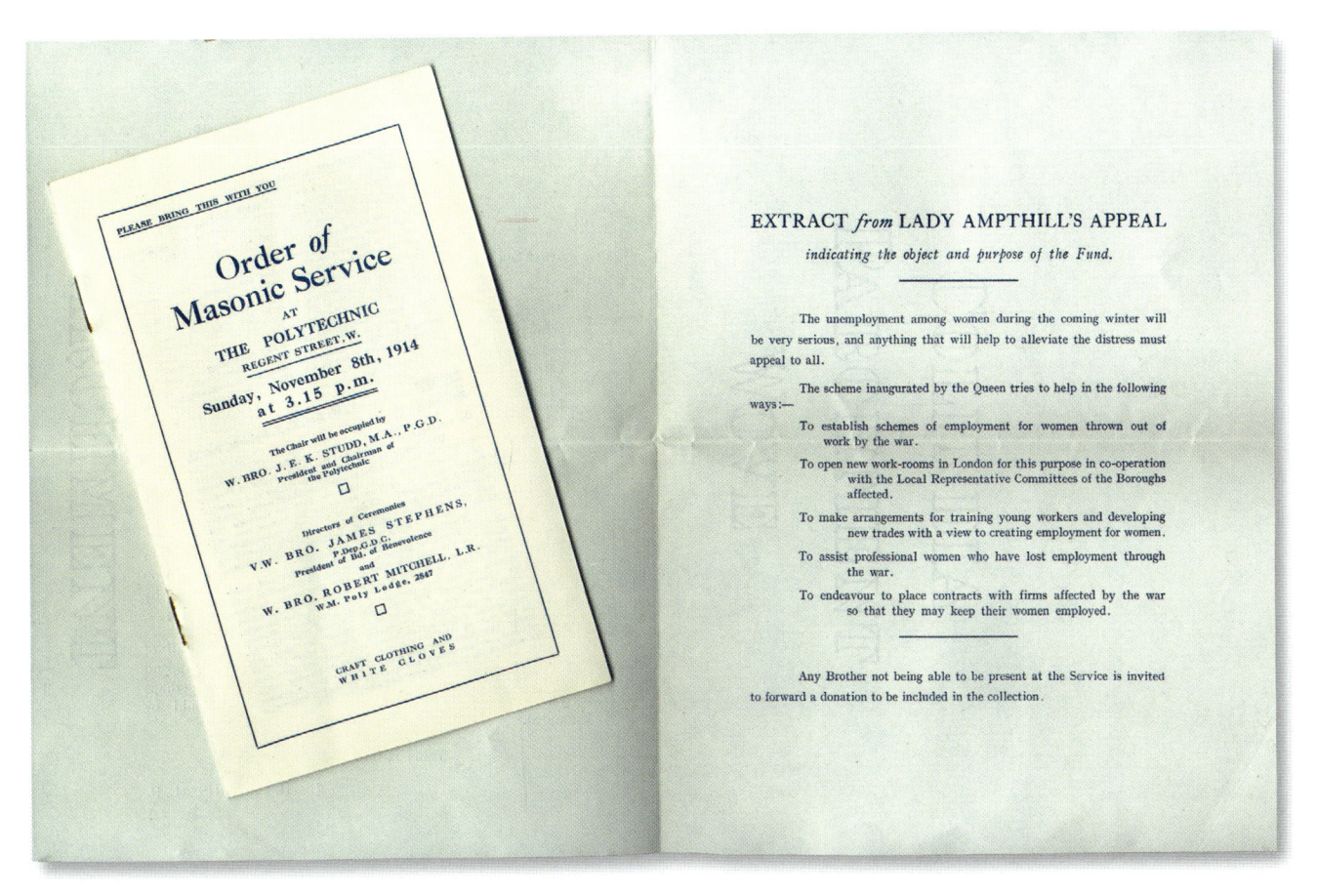

Memorial Fund. After financing a memorial to Kitchener at All Souls Chapel, St Paul's Cathedral, the Fund established Kitchener University Scholarships for servicemen to attend British universities after the war.

Another cause to benefit was the Blinded Soldiers' and Sailors' Hostel, later known as St Dunstan's, founded by Arthur Pearson, a newspaper magnate and entrepreneur who had lost his sight in 1913. Before March 1920, Grand Lodge sent approximately £200 raised by members' donations to this charity, which helped blinded soldiers and sailors to regain confidence and self-esteem, including a former pupil at the Boys' School. Harold Flett was assisted by St Dunstan's following his return to England, after losing his sight at the Dardanelles on in June 1915. Writing to *The Masonian* that December, Flett mentioned his employment at the United Yeast Company, Clerkenwell, reporting that, 'I have done far better than I expected. My shorthand speed has proved quite sufficient and my typewriting has been well up to the mark. Indeed, I have on two occasions been described as the best typist in this office… I feel quite justified in saying that I have proved of some worth to the firm, and not a mere war curiosity.' Grand Lodge also donated £105 to the Lord Roberts Memorial Workshops for Disabled Soldiers and Sailors, which had originated as the Soldiers and Sailors Help Society.

Donations for such causes were raised by members at home and abroad, with individual lodges raising significant amounts for local and national causes, contributions for the latter often being collected centrally by Grand Lodge. The efforts of just one lodge stand as an example of what many achieved. Royal Denbigh Lodge No.1143 raised over £21 between 1914 and 1918 for local and central war-related charities, in addition to sending £50 to the Masonic charities and investing £150 in National War Bonds. Its smaller local donations included £4 for cigarettes and tobacco for soldiers serving at the front in the 4th (Denbighshire) Battalion of the Royal Welch Fusiliers and the Denbighshire and Flintshire Prisoners of War Funds, while 'business as usual' donations of £10 were sent on five separate occasions to the RMIG, the RMIB and the RMBI.

Many lodges provided hospitality and entertainment for wounded soldiers hospitalised locally. Williamson Lodge No. 949 hosted a tea party at the Masonic Hall in Sunderland in the summer of 1916 for 50 wounded soldiers. The nine lodges in and around Rochdale provided entertainment at the Rochdale

LEFT Arthur Stanley MP, President of the British Red Cross Society 1914-43, shown here as the Provincial Grand Master of West Lancashire 1910-19.

BELOW Old Boys from the School at Bushey on Commemoration Day, 20 June 1914.

RIGHT Front page of The Masonian December 1914, the first edition after the declaration of war.

Empire, followed by tea at the town hall for about 750. In Huddersfield, five lodges supplemented the food at a 300-bed military hospital with a meat or fish breakfast at a cost of £45 per month. All the lodges in the district built and equipped a gymnasium at the Huddersfield War Hospital. Nottinghamshire Freemasons contributed a hut at Clipstone Camp, near Mansfield, Nottinghamshire, for the use of wounded hospital patients from the colonies. The recreation hut was opened by the Reverend Hayman on 8 September 1916, recognising the 'true friendship that has brought our colonists to fight for the old Motherland'. An orthopaedic pavilion at Derbyshire Hospital was provided by local Freemasons and several ambulances were provided for the front.

The Provincial Grand Lodge of Worcestershire established its own war relief fund in March 1916, under the auspices of the Provincial Grand Master, Sir William Campbell, who presided over a grand concert to raise funds. The Province had collected £1,400 by 1918. London freemasons set up a scheme, operated by the London Rank Association, to visit hospitalised sailors and soldiers in the metropolitan area.

Despite initial concerns about the effect of the war upon the Masonic and other charities, an aggregate total of over £167,000 was raised in 1916. Speaking at an event to commemorate Grand Lodge's bicentenary in 1917, the Deputy Grand Master, Sir Thomas Halsey, noted that the three Masonic institutions:

> … have all advanced and are advancing by leaps and bounds, even through these troublous times and have been enabled not only to continue but to increase their good and beneficial work.

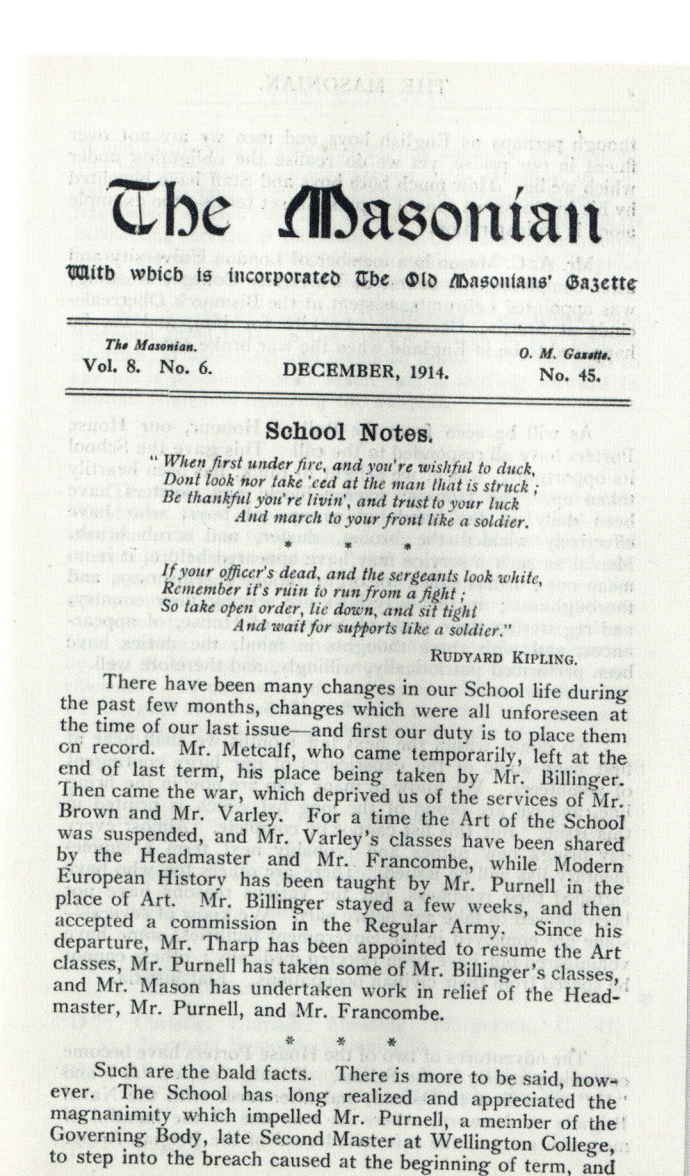

The Board of Benevolence made annual contributions to various causes of more than £100,000 in 1917, compared with £81,000 immediately before the war. The total for 1918-19 was more than £400,000.

This remarkable increase in disposable charitable income enabled Grand Lodge to consider new initiatives. In 1911, Percy Still and other members of Malmesbury Lodge No. 3156 in London had proposed the establishment of a Masonic nursing home and within two years the idea had the support of Grand Lodge. After the outbreak of war, the plans changed as Grand Lodge decided the initiative should

BELGIAN MASONIC RELIEF FUND.

4 & 5 COPTHALL COURT,
LONDON, E.C.

1st *February*, 1916.

Dear Sir and W. Bro.,

In July last we ventured to bring to your notice the above Fund, which has been inaugurated with the object of doing something to alleviate the distress amongst the Belgian Freemasons now resident in this country, and those still remaining in their native land. We invited you to bring this appeal before the members of your Lodge, in order that they might have an opportunity of participating in this work if its aims and objects appealed to them.

We are happy to be able to inform you that the result attained may be considered encouraging, in view of the multiplicity of charitable funds for which appeal has recently been made. Thanks, in a large measure, to the generosity of our Brethren in Victoria and Melbourne, the subscriptions received to date amount to over £800.

The policy of the Committee has been to afford regular assistance to a limited number of deserving cases, rather than to dissipate the fund in indiscriminate doles, and it is hoped that the steady flow of subscriptions will make it possible to continue this assistance until the end of the War. Various sums have also been remitted to Brussels towards the support of the work which is being carried on by Belgian Freemasons there in providing cheap meals for the more necessitous Brethren and their families. The Committee is entirely satisfied that this is a most excellent work, and that the funds remitted reached their destination, and are being wisely and carefully administered.

To maintain the fund—even on its present modest scale of activity—further subscriptions are required, and the Committee hopes that you will be so good as to bring this matter once more before the members of your Lodge.

The Committee desires to take this opportunity of expressing their gratitude to those Lodges who have already contributed, and to express the hope that the Lodges which in July last were not in a position to contribute to the fund may now be willing to take some share, however small, in this most beneficent work.

Contributions may be sent to the Treasurer direct, to one of the Honorary Secretaries, or to any member of the Committee.

Yours sincerely and fraternally,

Edward ROEHRICH, P.G.W. (Gᵉ Lᵉ Nationale de France), P.D.G.D.C. (England),
4 & 5 Copthall Court, London, E.C., *Chairman*.

Hon. Treasurer: Edmund HEISCH, J.G.W. (Gᵉ Lᵉ Nationale de France), P.G.D. (England),
2 St. Helen's Place, London, E.C.

Wm. P. ROWLANDS, L.R., Stock Exchange, London, E.C.
G. SMETS-MONDEZ, P.M.,
48 Leyborne Park, Kew Gardens, London, S.W.
} *Joint Hon. Secretaries.*

ABOVE Leaflet about the Belgian Masonic Relief Fund.

LEFT Founder's jewel of Lux in Tenebris Lodge No. 3856, *c.* 1918. Its members were associated with societies for the blind.

RIGHT Parianware bust of Henry Horatio Kitchener, Earl Kitchener of Khartoum, who was appointed Secretary of State for War in August 1914. Kitchener had been introduced to Freemasonry by the Duke of Connaught and initiated in Egypt in the 1880s.

focus on running the former Chelsea Women's Hospital at 237 Fulham Road, London, which was to be known as the Freemasons' War Hospital.

The hospital – classified as a Primary, or, Class A, facility by the War Office, suitable for receiving wounded men direct from the trenches – accepted a first convoy of patients soon after its official opening on 6 September 1916 and its initial 60-bed capacity soon increased to 77. Donations were received from many sources: members serving in the navy, in Mesopotamia, in the trenches, and from ships' captains in the Port of Archangel. The District Grand Lodge of Japan held a concert to raise money, the District Grand Lodge of Bengal raised almost £2,000 and the Grand Lodge of Victoria and other Grand Lodges across the world expressed solidarity for Masonic brethren by sending donations. However, the most unexpected contribution to the Freemasons' War Hospital came from interned members at the camp at Ruhleben, who contributed two marks each, sending a cheque for £15.

Although running the hospital proved more expensive than anticipated, it was a popular cause. Surplus funds enabled the hospital committee to occupy and run Cliff House at Caversham, near Reading, as a convalescent nursing home. In April 1918, the Bishop of London, Arthur Winnington-Ingram, offered Fulham Palace, with the sanction of

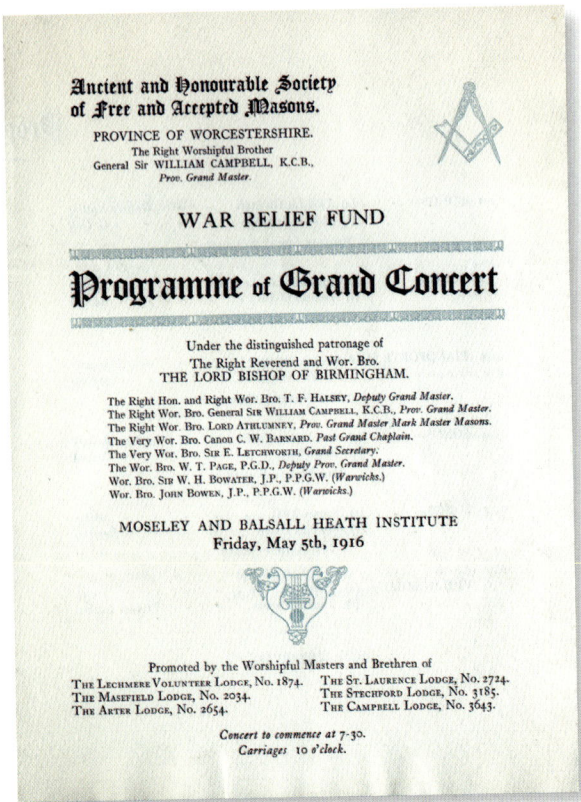

ABOVE An ambulance funded by Cornish Freemasons, one of several supported by different provinces.

LEFT Grand Concert programme May 1916, in aid of the Worcestershire War Relief Fund.

the War Office, to the British Red Cross Society. This was placed at the disposal of the Freemasons War Hospital and equipped as a second facility.

Masonic support for servicemen at the hospital included 'little gifts of creature comforts, promises for motor-drives, concert-parties, means of amusement and recreation'. The President of the Board of General Purposes, Alfred Robbins, took a keen interest in the hospital and his wife attended working parties to raise funds. In November 1916 Queen Amelia of Portugal inspected the hospital and took tea with Lady Letchworth, Mrs Alfred Robbins and Mrs James Stephens, respectively the wives of the Grand Secretary,

APRONS, ARMS AND ALMS: MASONIC CHARITY AND THE WAR

ABOVE Photograph of the orthopaedic pavilion at Derbyshire hospital, funded by local Freemasons.

RIGHT Portrait of Percy Still wearing a Permanent Stewards jewel.

the President of the Board of General Purposes and the President of the Board of Benevolence.

King George V and Queen Mary visited the Hospital that December. Bertha Sanders sent a report to *Massonica* about Christmas at the Freemasons' War Hospital, where wards were decorated with coloured paper and flowers made by disabled men. The first floor landing and one of the wards, decorated to represent Japan, won a prize. Another ward represented Italy, with oranges and lemons made of paper and grapes in bunches, and one small ward had a shrine in memory to the fallen. Ten VADs went round singing carols with a lantern and staff managed

THE FREEMASON—11th NOVEMBER, 1916.

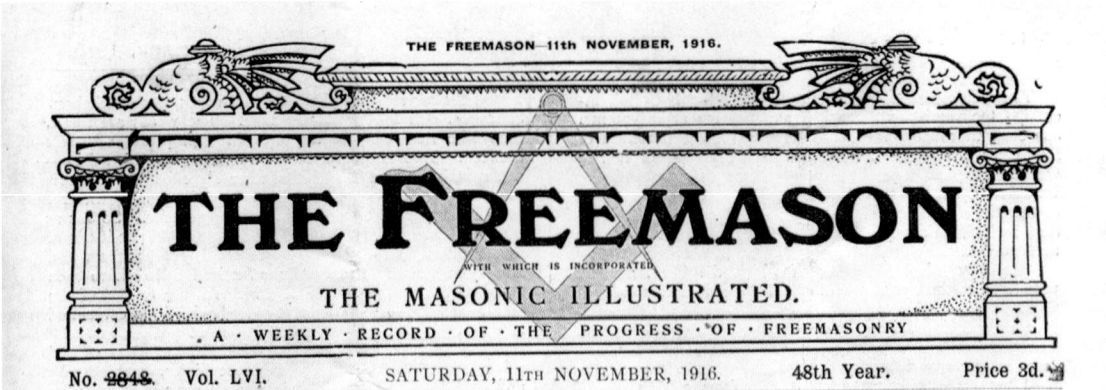

THE FREEMASON
WITH WHICH IS INCORPORATED
THE MASONIC ILLUSTRATED.
A · WEEKLY · RECORD · OF · THE · PROGRESS · OF · FREEMASONRY

No. 2848.   Vol. LVI.   SATURDAY, 11TH NOVEMBER, 1916.   48th Year.   Price 3d.

FREEMASONS WAR HOSPITAL
AND MASONIC NURSING HOME.

THE scheme for establishing the Freemasons War Hospital as a development of the proposal for a Masonic Nursing Home has advanced with remarkable rapidity, and its success up to the present is an evidence of the readiness with which members of the Craft respond to a cause that presents a two-fold appeal to patriotism and charity.

It will be remembered that the inaugural meeting of this new enterprise took place at the Mansion House last July, under the presidency of the Lord Mayor. It was then announced that the Masonic Nursing Home Committee had conceived the plan of establishing immediately a Freemasons War Hospital, to be offered to the War Office, for a suggested period of two years, this Hospital to be converted in due time into the Masonic Nursing Home, towards whose establishment the Committee has been working. It was stated at this meeting that the late premises of the well-known Chelsea Hospital for Women, 237, Fulham Road, S.W., had been secured for two years at a moderate rental, with an option to purchase the freehold at a very reasonable price.

The Committee's scheme at once received the cordial support of the Pro Grand Master, Bro. Lord Ampthill, who expressed the opinion that "this scheme will be unhesitatingly accepted and handsomely supported by the Craft, for the ultimate transition from a War Hospital to a permanent Nursing Home is a proposal which appeals to the imagination, and seems to hold great possibilities for good." The Deputy Grand Master, Bro. the Right Hon. T. F. Halsey, and Bro. the Hon. Arthur Stanley, M.P., Provincial Grand Master of West Lancashire, and Chairman of the Executive Committee of the British Red Cross Society, also welcomed the proposal with approval. The Committee duly offered the proposed Hospital, fully equipped, to the War Office (through the British Red Cross Society), and it was at once accepted. It was decided that the building, while in use for this purpose, should be designated "The Freemasons War Hospital" in order that the Masonic Fraternity might become identified in this way with a national need that was of urgent character; and thus a very useful enterprise was undertaken in the interval which must elapse before the achievement of the ultimate object of the Committee — the establishment of a permanent Nursing Home for the benefit of Brethren of the Craft.

The Institution has as its Chairman Bro. Charles E. Keyser, P.G.W., Deputy Prov. Grand Master of Hertfordshire, who is also one of the three Trustees, the other two being Bro. the Hon. A. Dudley Ryder, P.G.W., and Bro. Sir Charles Cheers Wakefield, Lord Mayor of London, J.G.W. The Hon. Treasurer of the movement is Bro. Sir Horace Marshall, P.G. Treas.; Bro. J. D. Langton, P.G.D., is the Hon. Solicitor, Bro. Arthur F. Whinney, P.G.D., is the Hon. Auditor, and the Joint Hon. Secretaries are Bro. Percy Still, P.G.D., and Bro. C. H. Thorpe, L.R. The Chairman of the Committee controlling the Hospital is Bro. George F. Marshall, P.A.G.D.C.

The equipment of the premises was undertaken without delay. Bro. A. Burnett Brown, Grand Superintendent of Works, who had already inspected the building and given the opinion that the offer was an exceptionally good bargain, personally supervised the necessary decorations and alterations; while in the furnishing and other equipment of the Hospital Bro. George F. Marshall gave invaluable assistance, only possible because of his unique experience of hospital work and requirements. During this very busy month of preparation the Hon. Treasurer and the Hon. Secretaries were constantly at the Hospital giving their time in its interests.

FREEMASONS WAR HOSPITAL: FRONT VIEW.

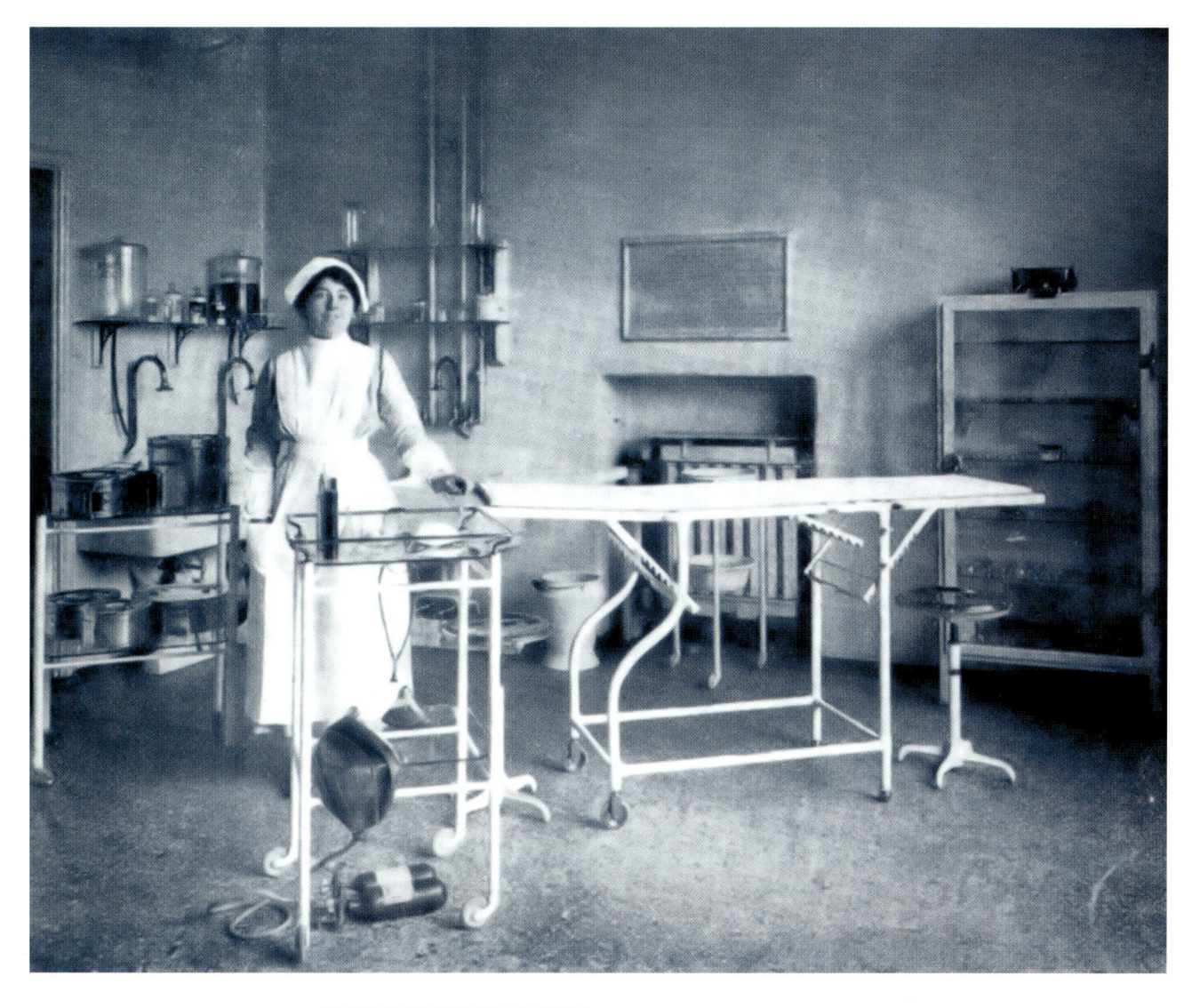

ABOVE Operating theatre at the Freemasons' War Hospital.

RIGHT Founder's jewel for Malmesbury Lodge No. 3156.

LEFT One of the many articles about the Freemasons' War Hospital in the Masonic Press.

to find turkeys to cook. Every worker at the hospital received a present from Father Christmas and every patient had a stocking.

The Freemasons' War Hospital facilities treated over 4,000 members of the armed forces in total during the war. Arthur Stanley as Chairman of the Red Cross Executive Committee stated with satisfaction that 'of the 14,000 to 15,000 hospitals under the control of the Red Cross Society, none excels the one provided by the Freemasons'. Grand Lodge had made a decision by September 1917 to purchase the Fulham-based hospital, in order to convert it into a Masonic facility. The premises had re-opened as the Freemasons' Hospital and Nursing

Home by autumn 1919, providing care for 46 in-patients who had to be Freemasons, their wives or dependent children. An extension fund was launched in 1929 to raise endowment funds to ensure that the hospital, later known as the Royal Masonic Hospital, was self-supporting.

Donations to the hospital were recognised by the award of the Permanent Stewards jewel. The jewel was first issued in silver, engraved on the reverse with the donor's name and lodge number, but later versions were made of base metal and often not inscribed. The design, by C.L.J. Doman (who also produced the Armistice Anniversary medal in 1928), showed humanity succouring the sick, a five-pointed star and the interlaced letters 'FH' for 'Freemasons' Hospital'. The motto was 'Aegros Sanat Humanitas' or 'Kindness Heals the Sick'. Its ribbon was in the dark and light blue of Craft Masonry.

The RMIB rules were updated in spring 1916 so that 54 candidates, whose fathers had died in the war, were admitted without ballot. As the war progressed, additional beneficiaries sought assistance from the RMBI in many cases where sons serving with the forces were no longer able to support elderly parents. The RMBI supported 1230 annuitants in 1915, adding a further 61 beneficiaries in the following year. The RMIG established a King Edward VII Memorial Fund to support up to 200 girls who lost fathers or

APRONS, ARMS AND ALMS: MASONIC CHARITY AND THE WAR

FACING PAGE Matron and VAD helpers.

LEFT Permanent Steward's jewel for the Royal Masonic Hospital.

RIGHT Programme for fundraising concert, Christmas 1917.

whose fathers had been incapacitated. By late 1918, 170 nominations were taken up, some attending the school while others chose to receive support while living at home. The governing committees sent special congratulations to everyone for the 'splendid discipline of the whole school under a most trying ordeal'.

Without doubt all the charities worked hard, and generally successfully, to maintain 'business as usual' for the duration of hostilities and with the financial support of members in English lodges and across the world. The author and Freemason Albert Calvert noted:

> …from the moment of the outbreak of War…the adventure upon which the Empire was launched produced an immediate and phenomenal response from all classes of the community – a community composed of those who serve and those who give and those who do both…in an age in which giving has become almost the most conspicuous trait in our national character, the Freemasons have worthily upheld their reputation for giving quickly and with both hands.

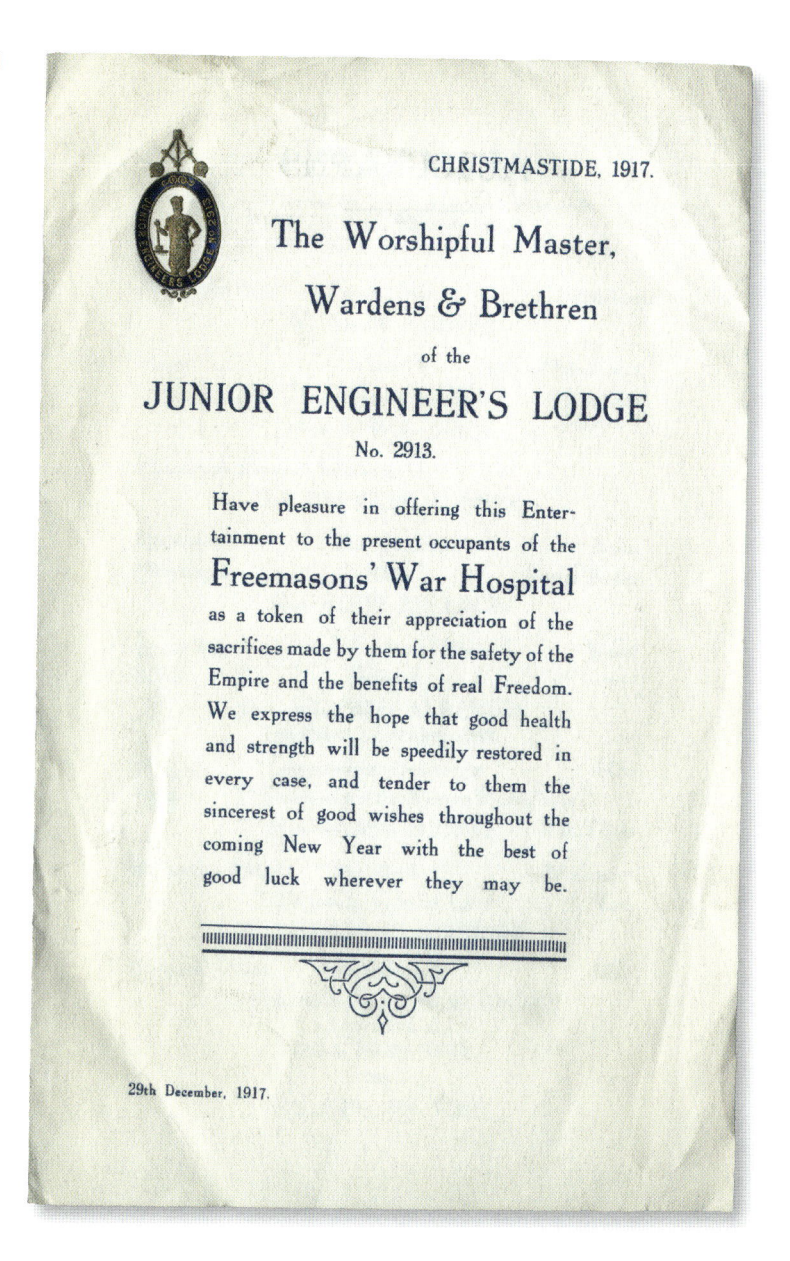

CHRISTMASTIDE, 1917.

The Worshipful Master, Wardens & Brethren of the JUNIOR ENGINEER'S LODGE No. 2913.

Have pleasure in offering this Entertainment to the present occupants of the Freemasons' War Hospital as a token of their appreciation of the sacrifices made by them for the safety of the Empire and the benefits of real Freedom. We express the hope that good health and strength will be speedily restored in every case, and tender to them the sincerest of good wishes throughout the coming New Year with the best of good luck wherever they may be.

29th December, 1917.

6

'THE IDEA SHOULD BE ENOUGH WITHOUT TRAPPINGS'

In September 1919, Major General Sir David Watson, the officer commanding the 4th Canadian division and a Past Deputy Grand Master of Quebec, presented to the Grand Lodge in London a gavel and block made from the oak beam of the now ruined cathedral at Ypres. It was a poignant presentation as Canadian soldiers had made a particularly significant contribution to the Third Battle of Ypres, otherwise known as 'Passchendaele'. It remains on permanent display in the Library and Museum there.

In the discussion between the clergyman and the Officer of Engineers in Kipling's short story 'In the Interests of the Brethren' set during the war, the officer talks about a Masonic meeting in a ruined church in Flanders where the members 'took a lot of trouble to make our regalia out of camouflage-stuff that we'd pinched, and we manufactured our jewels from old metal' to contradict the clergyman's view that 'the idea should be enough without trappings'. During and after the war, the creation of improvised items and works of art from what surrounded servicemen in the battle zones created a body of objects now known collectively as 'trench art', a term which has come to include items made out of war materials such as shell cases or bullets. Freemasons in the services improvised objects for use in everyday life from what they found around them, but they also created some items specifically for Masonic use.

In several lodges based in Britain, war materials were appropriated and incorporated into lodge fittings. The Aeronautical Inspection Directorate (AID) was created to design and refine aeroplane designs. Its members came from many locations, but its Chief Inspector Brigadier Ralph Bagnall-Wild realised that enough of them were Freemasons to make a lodge possible and through it create friendships between men who had never met before. The lodge they formed in 1917, originally to be called Aerinspect Lodge, was Ad Astra Lodge No. 3808. Its name, meaning 'to the stars', was inspired by the motto of the Royal Flying Corps. The imagery on the lodge's jewel included a rotary engine and a biplane.

The work of the AID was also directly represented in its collecting box, which was made from the central section of a laminated wood aircraft propeller. The serial marks were left on this and allowed the

ABOVE Founder's jewel for Ad Astra Lodge No. 3808.

LEFT Ypres gavel block presented by Major General Sir David Watson.

identification of the plane as an SE2B – an experimental design with a propeller to the rear rather than the front, which saw much service in the war. The large wooden marquetry tracing boards of the lodge carried this aviation theme still further by being mounted on propellers and engine camshafts. Even the stands for the banners used in the lodge were engine parts, thus surrounding the working lodge with emblems of its past achievements. The lodge closed in 2000, but its tracing boards continue in use by Royal Air Force Lodge No. 7335.

A similar link between trench art and function occurred in Royal Naval Anti-Aircraft Lodge No. 3790, where all the officers were deployed in action against German air raids by aeroplane or airship. The lodge officers' jewels were all made from Zeppelin duralumin (salvaged from the immense framework of downed Zeppelins and widely sold as souvenirs to aid the war effort), with a reserve supply retained for future needs – a later chaplain's jewel was made from this as well. The lodge jewel was based on the cap badge of a petty officer. The lodge's own copy of its history also had a military aspect, being covered in the fabric from an aeroplane, and the lodge collecting box was made from the case of an anti-aircraft shell, bearing the locations of the batteries of the unit after April 1918 when they relocated from London to Kent. The lodge was conscious of this use of materials and, at a meeting in November 1918, shortly before the Armistice, put on a display of 'war relics' which it intended to use to form the nucleus of a lodge museum.

Re-use of shell parts was prevalent in trench art, despite being illegal. Armament Lodge No. 3898, formed in 1918 by men involved with the Ministry of Munitions, used shell caps to fashion their collecting box and gavels. Once again, the metal for their jewels was appropriate. It was silver extracted from the lead ore used to make shrapnel shells.

There are relatively few examples of Masonic trench art provably made and used in a war zone, but the gavel of St Catherine's Park Lodge No. 2899 is the most potent example of this. The head was carved from the wooden parts of a German Mauser rifle found in a captured trench by the New Zealand Expeditionary Force, and the gavel itself was used in meetings held within the combat area. It passed to the St Catherine's Park Lodge in the 1920s because of that lodge's hospitality to overseas military Masons during the war. Improvised lodges often found ingenious ways to provide their working tools. The Aegean Lodge of Instruction was formed in Mudros on the Greek Island of Lemnos from the Freemasons of the Garrison and Fleet. It was conceived by two members of Phoenix Lodge No. 257 serving there. The working tools and lodge fittings were mainly designed by W. Bro Joliffe (the Dockyard Foreman), and were all made by voluntary effort under his supervision on board the repair ship HMS *Reliance* and in the aircraft repair shops ashore. The lodge met in a signal hut and all the fittings had to be removed between meetings. The Master and Wardens' pedestal covers were made from canvas and could be thrown over a conveniently-shaped table to form a complete set of lodge furniture that was easy to store between meetings. Masons of all regular constitutions met in this lodge. The lodge fittings are preserved in the Masonic Hall in Old Portsmouth and, in accordance with the wishes of the original members, are used at the November meeting of Phoenix Lodge No. 257 in memory of the Armistice of 1918.

Freemasons also gathered non-military items from the areas where they were stationed. An ancient Egyptian maul found in a tomb in Memphis, Egypt, at the start of the war in December 1914 by Major William Peart Thomas – a past member of Pegasus Lodge No. 2205, Athlumney Lodge No. 3245 and the Royal Army Medical Corps – found its way back to England and was mounted with engraved silver bands to explain its origin. Troops stationed in Jerusalem found themselves near to the legendary quarries of King Solomon and so returned with fragments of rock that they felt gave them a physical link to the stonemasons of Solomon's Temple. This was in a wider tradition of 'souveniring' which became prevalent in the war.

ABOVE Ad Astra Lodge No. 3808 collecting box and gavels, made from an aircraft propeller.

ENGLISH FREEMASONRY AND THE FIRST WORLD WAR

'THE IDEA SHOULD BE ENOUGH WITHOUT TRAPPINGS'

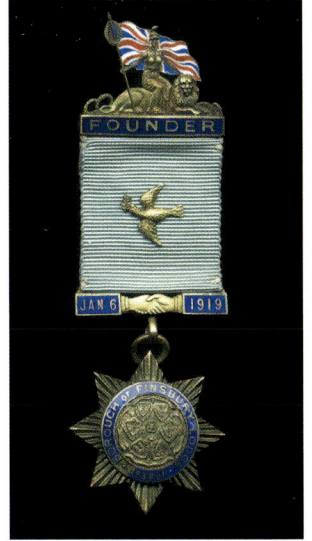

ABOVE Founding Deacon's jewel for Borough of Finsbury Lodge No. 3901.

ABOVE Founder's jewel of Victory Lodge No. 3986.

ABOVE Founder's jewel of Lodge of Remembrance No. 4037.

ABOVE Founder's jewel of New Era Lodge No. 4057.

The aftermath of the war saw lodges formed to commemorate both peace and victory. The Borough of Finsbury Lodge No. 3901 was named after the local London area with which its early members were associated but its warrant was issued within days of the Armistice, so the lodge jewel patriotically included a figure of Britannia and an English lion. The jewel of Victory Lodge No. 3986 in Newcastle upon Tyne, established in 1919, depicted Britannia crowning the British 'Tommy' with a wreath of laurels. More soberly, the jewel of the Lodge of Remembrance No. 4037, established in December 1919 and consecrated in February 1920, depicted the plaster and wood Cenotaph in Whitehall designed by Sir Edwin Lutyens. The permanent Cenotaph made of Portland stone was only unveiled in November 1920. The jewel of New Era Lodge No. 4057 in Kingston upon Thames (also 1920) showed a child being raised up to the new light of dawn. Both these lodges also chose names to reflect the spirit of the times.

Although no further items of First World War trench art are recorded by Grand Lodge in the 1920s or 1930s, items continued to be presented within individual lodges. The Prince of Wales (later King Edward VIII) presented a maul made from part of Ypres Cathedral to Navy Lodge No. 2612 in 1923. That lodge also had a collecting box in the form of a rum tub made from the timber of HMS Iris II, a Liverpool ferry commandeered for the Royal Naval raid on Zeebrugge in 1918. Examples of Masonic trench art remain both in public collections and in individual lodges, acting as a physical reminder of the war that connect Freemasons of the twenty first century to their predecessors in a very practical way.

FACING PAGE TOP St. Catherine's Park Lodge No. 2899 gavel and box.

FACING PAGE BOTTOM LEFT Founding Steward's jewel for Armament Lodge No. 3898.

FACING PAGE BOTTOM RIGHT Ancient Egyptian maul.

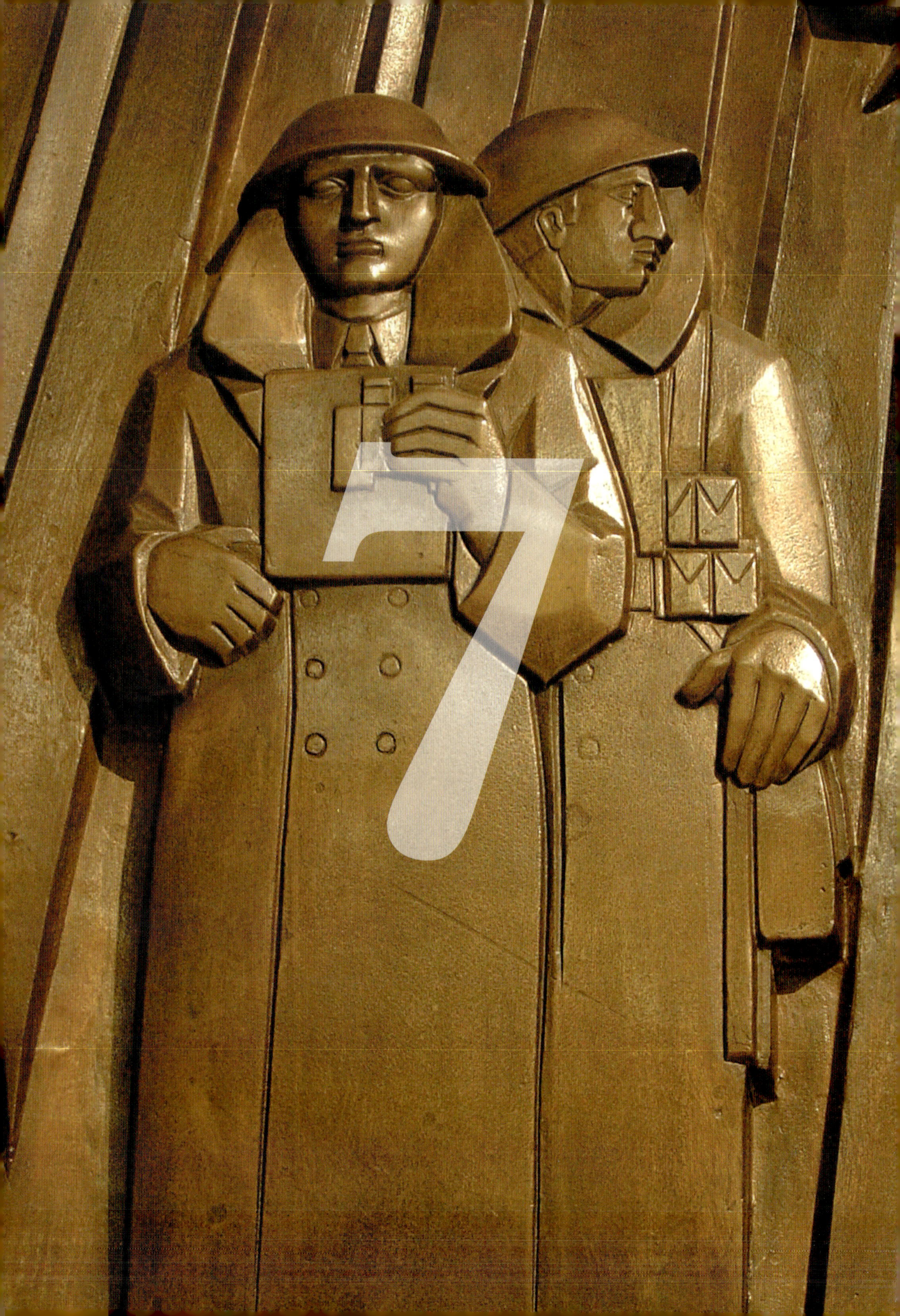
7

POST-WAR WORLD

On 27 June 1919, Lord Ampthill as Pro Grand Master presided over an Especial Grand Lodge at the Royal Albert Hall for the celebration of peace. Invitations to attend had been sent to the Grand Master and Grand Secretary of every English-speaking sovereign jurisdiction and amongst the audience of over 8,000 were representatives from Ireland, Scotland, 16 American states, several Canadian provinces and New Zealand.

During the meeting, the new American Ambassador to London, John W. Davis, was made Past Senior Grand Warden. It was agreed to present an address to King George V, which expressed a desire to work for peace: 'It is our earnest hope that with the help of God our worldwide and ancient fraternity may become more extensively serviceable to mankind and may be of material assistance in promoting every effort to secure peace on earth and good will among men'. The next day, the *Freemasons' Chronicle* described the occasion as unique and 'the exemplification of the Universality of Freemasonry'.

The formal meeting was part of a week of activities hosted by individual London lodges, including a Third Degree ceremony in Jubilee Masters Lodge No. 2712, presided over by Sir Henry McMahon, where the candidate was Commander Bryan Adams who had been involved in the Zeebrugge raid in 1918, visits to the Masonic schools and the Houses of Parliament, where a commemorative photograph was taken.

As early as the first Grand Lodge meeting held after the Armistice in December 1918, it had been noted that an incidental outcome of the war had been the increased amount of communication with Grand Lodges in other jurisdictions. In the post-war years there would be even more Grand Lodges. The Treaty of Versailles was signed on the day after the Especial Grand Lodge to mark the peace, 28 June 1919, exactly five years after the assassination of Archduke Franz Ferdinand.

It was the first in a series of treaties drawn up between the Allied Powers and Germany and its former allies. Amongst the principles which underlay these treaties was that of self-determination recognising national identities. The Treaty of Trianon, signed in 1920, created separate national states including Romania, Czechoslovakia and Yugoslavia. In due

ABOVE Pax Victoris Medal (Birmingham 1919).

RIGHT Glass engraved with the date of the Armistice.

course, Masonic lodges were established in each of these countries. The National Grand Lodge of Romania at Bucharest and the Grand Lodge of Yugoslavia at Belgrade were both 'recognised' by the English Grand Lodge in 1930, together with two Grand Lodges in Czechoslovakia, the German-speaking Grand Lodge *Lessing zu den drei Ringen* and the Czech-speaking National Grand Lodge of Czechoslovakia. Recognition was often followed by a visit by representatives to London and by presentations which, in the case of the National Grand Lodge of Czechoslovakia, included a set of Masonic jewels designed by the artist and Freemason Alphonse Mucha.

The Treaty of Versailles also established the League of Nations, an international organisation whose principal mission was to maintain world peace. The League administered a system of mandates by which control over former colonies and territories once administered by states defeated in the war was passed to other countries. Amongst the mandates received by Britain were those for Mesopotamia and Palestine. Britain had taken control of the oil fields near Basra in Mesopotamia (modern-day Iraq) by late 1914 to protect its interests, although it was not until March 1917 that the Ottoman army was decisively defeated and Baghdad captured. British army officers based in Baghdad petitioned for a new lodge; Lodge Mesopotamia No. 3820 was established in February 1918 with Lieutenant General Sir George MacMunn

POST-WAR WORLD

ABOVE Masonic visitors to the Peace Celebration in 1919, photographed at the Houses of Parliament. Ampthill is shown fifth from the left on the front row.

LEFT Trowel of Californian gold, silver and onyx presented by the Grand Lodge of California.

87

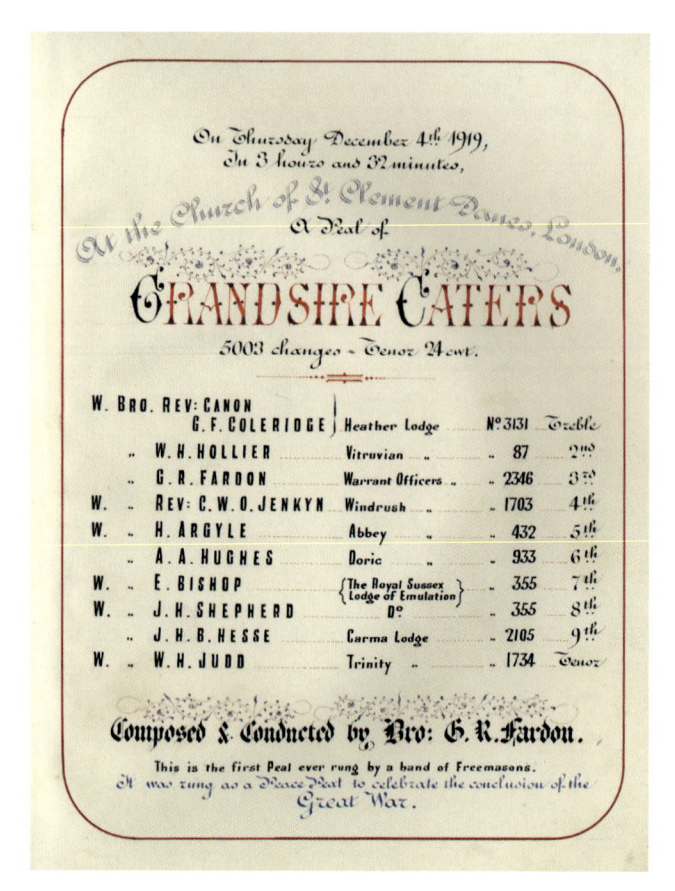

ABOVE Souvenir of the Peace Peal, 1919.

ABOVE Mucha jewels.

as its first Master. The lodge jewel depicted palm trees and camels. A second lodge, Baghdad Lodge No. 4022, was formed in 1919. Local unrest effectively ended the British mandate and led to the establishment of the Kingdom of Iraq in 1921, but with Britain retaining control of foreign and military policy. As commercial activities increased, four more British lodges were established including Lodge Babylonia No. 4326 for those involved in the oil production industry.

In December 1917, British and allied forces had captured Jerusalem from the Ottoman Empire and Britain was subsequently awarded the mandate to administer Palestine (comprising modern Israel, the West Bank and Gaza). In 1924, Philip Colville Smith, the Grand Secretary, led a delegation to Palestine where he inaugurated two new Masonic lodges, the Lodge of King Solomon's Temple No. 4611 and Lydda Lodge No. 4613. He returned there in 1930 to mark the formation of the Lodge of the Four Hills No. 5185 in Jerusalem, its name inspired by the location of the city. In his speech at the consecration of the first of these lodges, he emphasised its Masonic significance:

> To see you gathered here in this place which the whole legend of the Craft is associated [with]… is an auspicious event within annals of the Craft. Freemasonry through drawing on its main legend – and all its symbolism from the Temple [of Solomon] and its builders – [has] acted on [its] legitimate connection with the city [of] Jerusalem. This is the first English lodge under the jurisdiction of the Mother Grand Lodge of the World to meet permanently in Jerusalem.

ABOVE Founding Master's jewel for Lodge Mesopotamia No. 3820, worn by Lieutenant General Sir George MacMunn.

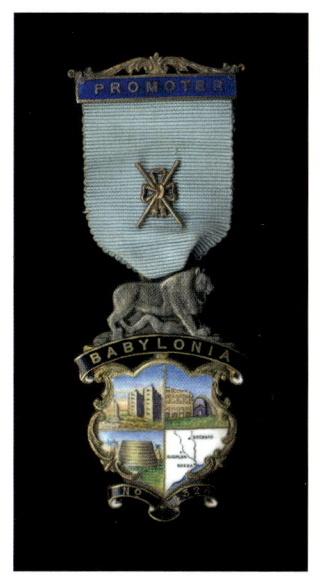

ABOVE Jewel for Lodge Babylonia No. 4326.

ABOVE Consecrating Master's jewel for the Lodge of King Solomon's Temple No. 4611, presented to Sir Philip Colville Smith.

ABOVE Founder's jewel for the Cologne Lodge of Instruction, 1923.

Sometimes a more informal approach was taken. At the end of the war, the British army in Germany became an army of occupation with its headquarters in Cologne. A Masonic society was formed there in 1921 which later adopted the name British Masonic Society in Rhineland. The society organised social events such as river trips and dances and made occasional donations to Masonic charities. It continued to meet until December 1923, when it was replaced by a lodge of instruction meeting under the sanction of a London lodge, Honour and Generosity No. 165. It moved to Wiesbaden with the army headquarters in 1925. Four years later the occupation of the Rhineland ended in accordance with the provisions of the Treaty of Versailles and the lodge of instruction closed. Its lodge furniture, some locally made, was transferred to Per Mare Per Terram Lodge of Instruction in Chatham, Kent.

Colville Smith's visit to Palestine was only one of a series of visits made by senior English Freemasons overseas in the 1920s and 1930s, in a conscious policy to strengthen the ties between London, overseas members and overseas grand lodges. The first visit was in April 1921, when Colville Smith travelled to Egypt to install the new District Grand Master for Egypt and the Sudan. Acknowledged as the first visit by a Grand Secretary to a District, the visit lasted eight days, during which the party from London attended six lodge meetings.

Several visits were made to Canada and to South America. A visit lasting six months and covering more than 25,000 miles was made to India, Burma and Ceylon in 1927-8, led by the Deputy Grand Master, Lord Cornwallis. In 1926, Colville Smith led a Masonic delegation on visits throughout Africa from Cape Town to Cairo during which the visitors attended 62 Masonic meetings.

Several new lodges reinforced these imperial links. The declared object of Motherland Lodge No. 3861, formed in London in the summer of 1918, was 'to weld together in closer union all the English-speaking people in all parts of the world, and more particularly their Imperial Commonwealth'.

Alfred Robbins, knighted in 1917, undertook an extensive and high-profile Masonic tour of the United States in 1924. Reporting to Grand Lodge on his return, he said, 'I returned with the full assurance that the American Freemasonry we recognise… is as true as English Masonry to the essential principles and tenets of the Craft.' With an estimated three million members, the Masonic strength of America was matching its increasing economic importance and Robbins' visit there was the first of several by senior Freemasons over the next 15 years.

A notable absence from this Grand Lodge diplomacy was Europe. The English Grand Lodge maintained its distance from European Freemasonry; the only European visits were to Sweden in 1932 and 1935, and briefly to Greece in 1938. Masonic relations with Austria had resumed in 1930 when the Grand Lodge of Vienna, a post-war creation with 14 lodges,

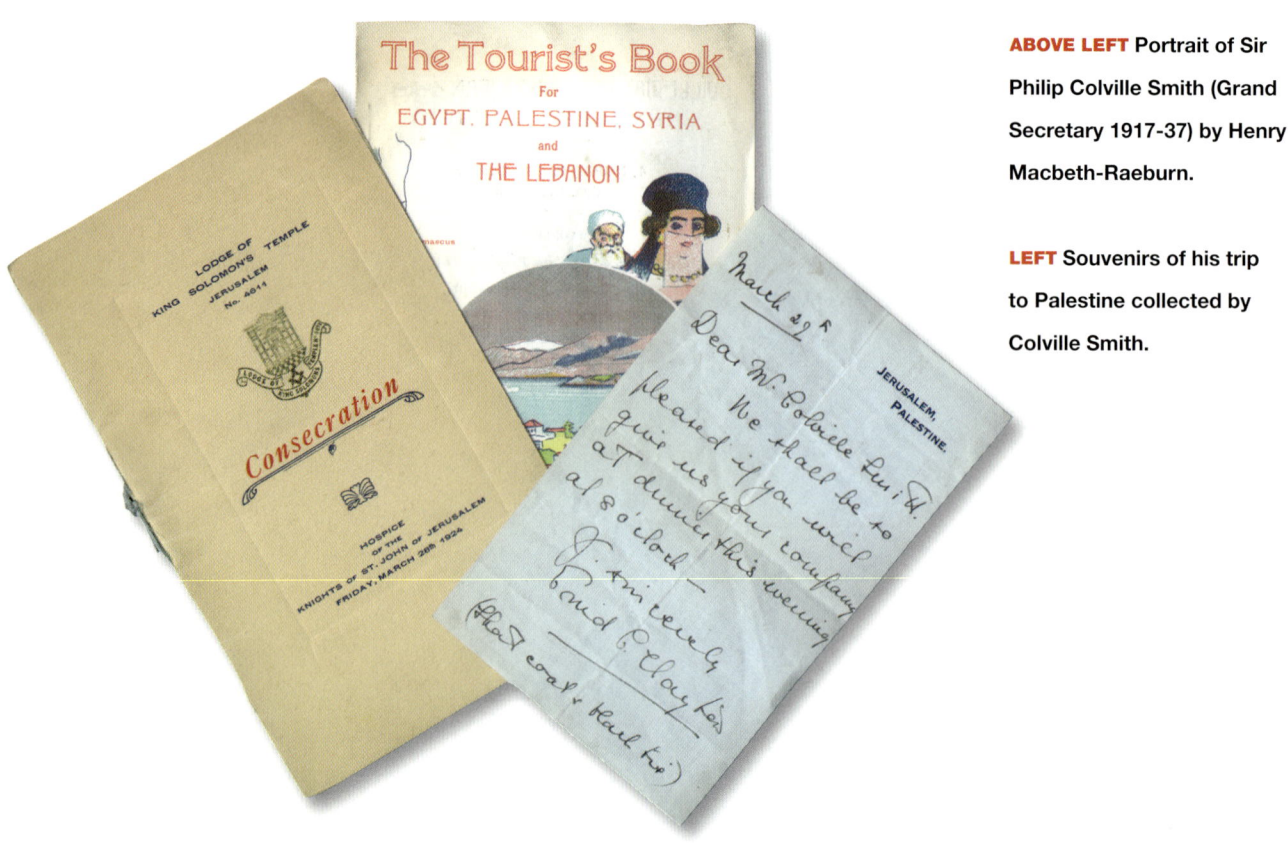

ABOVE LEFT Portrait of Sir Philip Colville Smith (Grand Secretary 1917-37) by Henry Macbeth-Raeburn.

LEFT Souvenirs of his trip to Palestine collected by Colville Smith.

LEFT Consecrating Master's jewel for Motherland Lodge No. 3861, presented to Sir Philip Colville Smith in 1918.

RIGHT Portrait of Fiennes Stanley Wykeham, 1st Baron Cornwallis, Deputy Grand Master 1926-35, by May Bridges Lee.

was recognised. The Masonic author Eugen Lennhoff attended the opening of the Peace Memorial in 1933, on behalf of that Grand Lodge. Relations with three German Grand Lodges were finally resumed in 1932.

The end of the war had also revived the idea of international associations of Freemasons. The first post-war congress of the Masonic International Association was held in Geneva in October 1921. It was attended by representatives from most continental European Grand Lodges, the Grand Lodge of New York and the Grand Orient of Turkey, but the English Grand Lodge ruled out attendance at a conference it considered to be political. Robbins took the opportunity to reiterate his call for a Masonic League of Nations, first made in July 1918, although this never moved towards formal establishment.

Another issue which faced the post-war Grand Lodge was the involvement of women in Freemasonry. Since 1912, the Grand Master of the Honourable Fraternity of Antient Masonry, one of the three English Masonic bodies then admitting women, had been Marion Lindsay Halsey. She was the daughter-in-law of Sir Frederick Halsey, the Deputy Grand Master and, like him, had guided her Grand Lodge through the war. Although the United Grand Lodge promptly re-stated in 1919 that: 'all such bodies which admit women to membership are clandestine and irregular', Marion Halsey petitioned for recognition. The absolute rejection of this approach by the Grand Secretary marked the start of her Fraternity limiting its membership to women.

English translations of *The Protocols of the Elders of Zion*, or, *The Protocols of the Meetings of the Learned Elders of Zion*, allegedly the minutes of a secret meeting of senior figures of world Jewry in which they discussed their plans for world domination, first appeared early in 1920. In Britain, the *Protocols* were presented as authentic in a series of articles in the *Morning Post* newspaper in July 1920, and then published in book form as *The Cause of World Unrest*, a copy of which was owned by the Grand Secretary, indicating Grand Lodge's concern about its allegations of a Judeo-

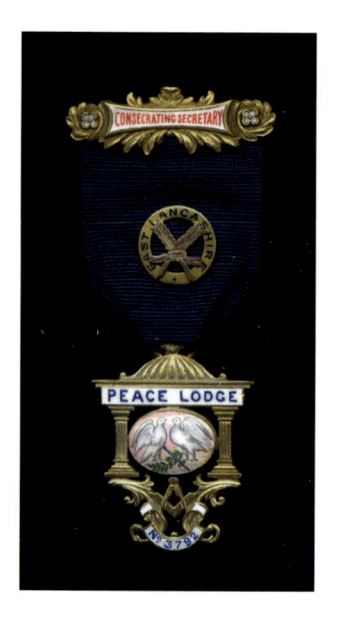

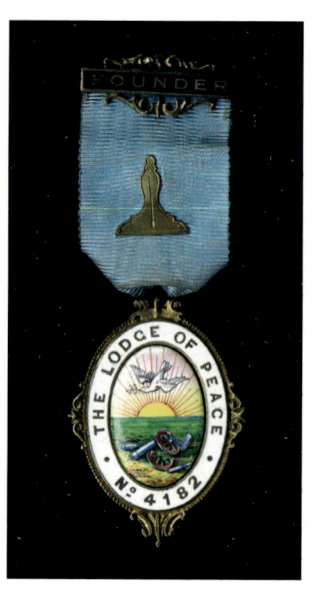

ABOVE LEFT Consecrating Secretary's jewel for Peace Lodge No. 3792, presented to Verney Clayton, 1917

ABOVE RIGHT Founding Senior Warden's jewel for Lodge of Peace No. 4182, presented to W.J. Handley, 1921

LEFT Colville Smith's copy of The Cause of World Unrest.

Masonic conspiracy. Three articles in *The Times* in 1921 exposed the *Protocols* as forgeries but they continued to be widely published.

In 1920, the English Grand Lodge issued a statement entitled Aims and Relationships of the Craft. This emphasised obedience to the law and allegiance to the state, the requirement for each member to believe in a Supreme Being and the prohibition on discussions of topics of a political or theological nature in lodges. The statement was a response to these contemporary events. It was a reaction to the establishment or revival of what were considered to be various 'irregular' Masonic bodies (including the women's Grand Lodges) who were making, according to Robbins, 'sedulous endeavours to induce Freemasons to join in their assemblies'. It also sought to overcome misapprehensions caused by the rise in post-war Europe of what London considered to be irregular Freemasonry involved in politics and issues such with anticlericalism.

The United Grand Lodge took the opportunity to emphasise its links with the Royal Family. In 1918, a new official seal was required and steps were taken to regularise the existing coat of arms design and add a 'Bordure' indicative of the Arms of England to mark the long association with Edward VII and other members of the Royal House. In July 1919, the *Freemasons' Chronicle* wrote about 'Our New Royal Brother', giving details of the membership of the Prince of Wales (later Edward VIII) in Household Brigade Lodge No. 2614. His brother Albert (later George VI) was to be initiated in the same lodge in

RIGHT Invitation to the initiation of the Duke of York (later King George VI.

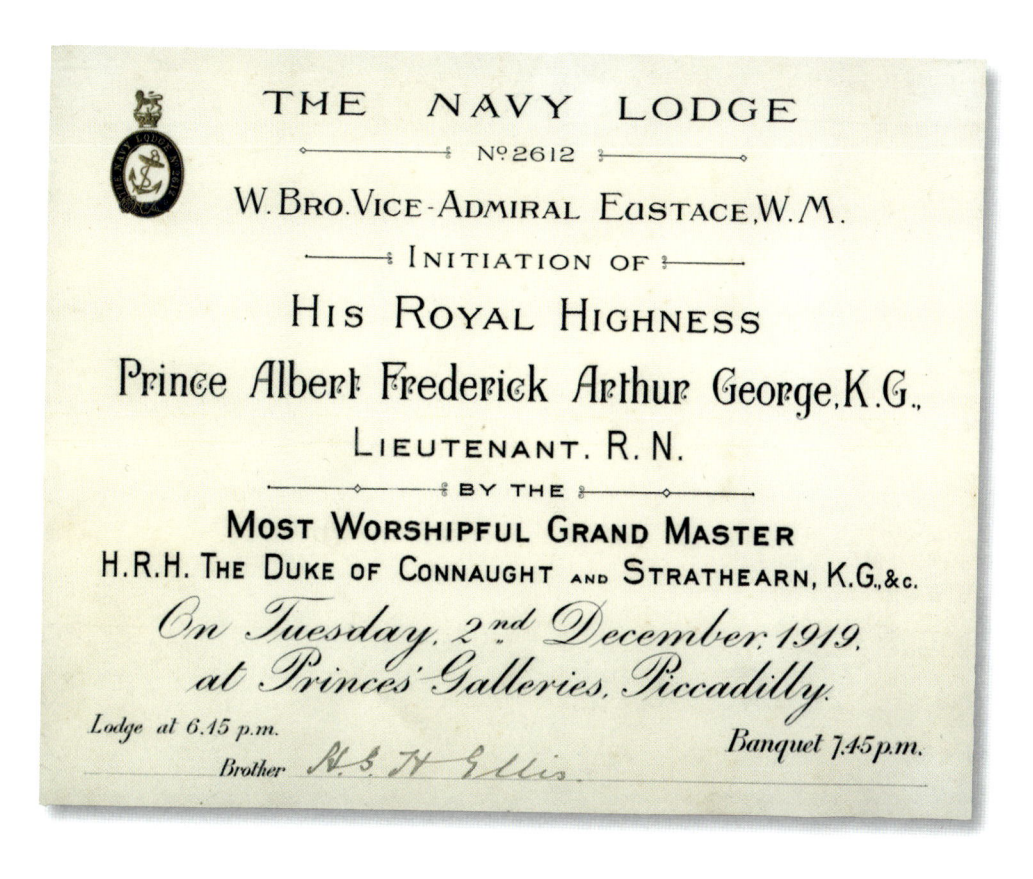

THE NAVY LODGE
Nº 2612
W. Bro. Vice-Admiral Eustace, W.M.
Initiation of
His Royal Highness
Prince Albert Frederick Arthur George, K.G.,
Lieutenant. R. N.
by the
Most Worshipful Grand Master
H.R.H. The Duke of Connaught and Strathearn, K.G., &c.
On Tuesday, 2nd December, 1919,
at Princes' Galleries, Piccadilly.
Lodge at 6.15 p.m. Banquet 7.45 p.m.
Brother H.S.H. Ellis

December 1919 and their younger brother George, Duke of Kent, in Navy Lodge No. 2612 in 1928.

The period following the end of the war saw a dramatic increase in the number of new candidates. Between 1917 and 1929, more than 1,300 new lodges were established to meet what Robbins described as an 'estimated doubling of the total membership'. In 1921, nearly 27,000 membership certificates were issued to new members, more than double the figure in 1913, which was itself a pre-war record. In the province of Essex alone, over 40 lodges were constituted between 1919 and 1929, and membership doubled to 8,800. A desire to continue comradeship, also reflected in the growth of veterans and comrades associations, was explained by Rudyard Kipling in 1926 in his fictional Lodge of Faith and Works, where Brother Burges' explanation of Freemasonry's attraction is that, 'All Ritual is fortifying. Ritual's a natural necessity for mankind. The more things are upset, the more they fly to it.'

Several of these new lodges took the opportunity to mark the spirit of the times in their name. Formed in 1917, Peace Lodge No. 3792 in Manchester anticipated the end of the war, while Pax Humana Lodge No. 3908 in London and Pax Magna Lodge No. 3916 in Nottingham were granted their warrants in December 1918 and January 1919. The jewel of the Lodge of Peace No. 4182, in London, showed a dove with an olive branch flying above a cannon against a sunlit background.

In 1918, the worldwide influenza epidemic was killing 7,000 people in Britain every week. Masonic records did not routinely record cause of death so the overall impact of the epidemic upon Freemasonry cannot be measured. One victim was the former Prince Louis of Battenberg who, in 1917, at the king's request and in the interests of 'Anglicising' the Royal family, had assumed for himself and his descendants the surname of Mountbatten. His death was noted in the Grand Lodge Proceedings. The *Freemasons' Chronicle*,

ABOVE Artist's impression of the new Freemasons' Hall in 1933

which continued to record casualties and their cause of death, gave details of several others including Edward Brookman, a Plumstead machinist aged 34 and a member of Woolwich Polytechnic Lodge No. 3578, and Francis Wicks, a former bank clerk and member of Doric Lodge No. 81 in Woodbridge, Suffolk, who died of flu in Warley Military Hospital at the age of 27. While all the girls at Clapham survived, a member of staff and former pupil at the school, May A. Downes, died, as did one of the domestic staff at Bushey.

Another challenge that post-war Freemasonry faced was how to deal with members and potential members who had been injured. Drawing their rules originally from the medieval period when a workman's physical imperfections would often have restricted his ability to work, the Masonic Antient Charges embodied the idea of a 'perfect youth'. This had already been relaxed in the 19th century to allow men who were blind or otherwise disabled to join provided they could comply with the various ceremonies. The war caused this issue to be considered again and explicit guidance was issued in 1918 that 'when the defect does not render a candidate incapable of learning our art, there is no reason why he should not be initiated'.

On Wednesday 19 July 1933, over 5,000 Freemasons led by the Grand Master, the Duke of Connaught, gathered at the new building in Great Queen Street for the dedication of the Masonic Peace Memorial. Amongst the speeches, orations and prayers was a message from King George V:

It is my earnest hope that this Hall may for ever stand as a monument to that public spirit and comradeship which united Freemasons to see that the names of their Brethren who made the supreme sacrifice in the Great War should never be forgotten.

NOTES ON SOURCES

This book represents the first attempt to review the impact of the 1914-18 War on English Freemasonry. The Proceedings of the Quarterly Communications of the United Grand Lodge of England, which are available in printed form in Masonic and deposit libraries, have provided an essential basis. They have been supplemented by other contemporary publications, particularly the two major Masonic newspapers of the periods, *The Freemason* and the *Freemasons' Chronicle*, and publications by the various Masonic charities. Letters and documents from the archives of the United Grand Lodge, especially the papers of Sir Alfred Robbins, President of the Board of General Purposes 1913-31, have been invaluable although the scope of this book has meant that only a small amount of this material has been used leaving room for further research on many of the war-time events and individuals. Sir Alfred Robbins' book, *English Speaking Freemasonry*, published in 1930, includes his account of the period. There are also accounts of the war's impact on individual lodges and chapters in their histories, and in provincial histories. These latter sources and the minutes on which they are based would also be a fruitful resource for further study.

BIBLIOGRAPHY

Amongst the other sources which shed light on the period covered by this book are:

Calderwood, Paul, *Freemasonry and the Press in the Twentieth Century: A National Newspaper study of England and Wales*, Farnham, 2013

Cowburn, Lorna, *Polished Cornerstones: A History of the Royal Masonic School for Girls 1788-2009*, Eastbourne, 2009

Daniel, James W., *Masonic Networks and Connections*, Melbourne, 2007

Dennis, Mark J. R. and Saunders, Nicholas J., *Craft and Conflict: Masonic Trench Art and Military Memorabilia*, London, 2003

Flynn, Keith, *Behind the Wire: An Account of Masonic Activity by Prisoners of War*, Cardiff, 2004

Hamill, John M., *And the Greatest of these is Charity: the Development of Masonic Charity*, Prestonian Lecture, London, 1993

Harland-Jacobs, Jessica L., Builders *of Empire: Freemasons and British Imperialism 1717-1927*, North Carolina, 2007

Hewitt, A. Reginald, *Craftsmen in Captivity (Masonic Activities of Prisoners of War)* Ars Quatuor Coronatorum, Volume 77, London 1965

Howe, Ellic, *The Collapse of Freemasonry in Nazi Germany*, Ars Quatuor Coronatorum, Volume 95, London 1973

Reuther, John, *Freemasonry and the Great War*, Ars Quatuor Coronatorum, Volume 111, London 1999

Smyth, Frederick, *The Master Mason at Arms*, Prestonian Lecture, London 1990